# Mary's Song

## Living Her Timeless Prayer

### Mary Catherine Nolan, O.P.

**ave maria press**   Notre Dame, Indiana

Mary Catherine Nolan, OP, is a theology teacher at the Dominican Ecclesial Institute in Albuquerque, New Mexico. In addition to her work as spiritual director, retreat preacher, and writer, Mary Catherine is concerned with issues of peace and justice. In 1984, as rural life director for the diocese of New Ulm, she was honored with an award from the Minnesota Catholic Conference for her work in promoting justice for farmers. In 1994 she received a doctorate in sacred theology from the International Marian Research Institute at the University of Dayton.

All scripture texts in this work, with the exception of Luke 1:46-55, are taken from the *New American Bible with Revised New Testament and Revised Psalms* © 1991, 1986, 1970 Confraternity of Christian Doctrine, Washington, D.C., and are used by permission of the copyright owner. All rights reserved. No part of the *New American Bible* may be reproduced in any form without permission in writing from the copyright owner.

International Standard Book Number:     0-87793-724-9 CB

0-87793-701-X PB

Cover and text design by Katherine Robinson Coleman

Printed and bound in the United States of America.

*Library of Congress Cataloging-in-Publication Data*
Nolan, Mary Catherine.
Mary's song : living her timeless prayer / Mary Catherine Nolan.
        p. cm.
    Includes bibliographical references.
    ISBN 0-87793-701-X (pbk.)
        1. Magnificat--Criticism, interpretation, etc. I. Title.
BS2595.52 .N65 2001
226.4'06--dc21                                              00-011092
                                                                        CIP

# Contents

Let Mary's soul be in each of you to proclaim the greatness of the Lord. Let her spirit be in each to rejoice in the Lord. The Lord is magnified, not because the human voice can add anything to God, but because he is magnified in us.

—St. Leo the Great

# Foreword

Mary Catherine Nolan portrays Mary as a person who "gathers in her arms" the *anawim*—the marginal people of history—and presents them to God. This book results in a touching, spiritual, and uplifting journey through the Hebrew and Christian scriptures. It captures the *kairos event* of ancient and modern peoples uniting them to God through their search for meaning in life.

Through the years the teaching church has described the Magnificat as a song praising and thanking God for the wondrous gifts bestowed upon Mary. God continues bestowing those wondrous gifts on the people of today. These accounts of personal experiences unite all generations of believers, confirming for us that God is a faithful God. This knowledge enables us to trust in hope that our faithful God will continually be with future generations (Psalms 103, 136, and Exodus 20).

Theologians and scripture scholars extol the Magnificat for the message it brings—a message of solidarity with the poor, as well as a message for social justice and liberation. Within the text are expressions coming from the Torah (the first five books of Hebrew scriptures), the Prophets, and the Writings. As a gift from Luke's gospel (Luke 1:46-55), it is an ideal prayer for a believer. No wonder then that the Magnificat is a good model for how to pray, and makes *Mary's Song* a prayerful experience for readers.

Even though this book is a writing on the spirituality of prayer, it is the result of five years of serious scholarly research. The research led to the author's doctorate in Marian Theology at the International Marian Research Institute in Dayton, Ohio. Her in-depth knowledge of this Marian prayer, combined with lively and personal experiences from her own life, provides the reader with a joyous presentation of the content of Mary's song.

There is a reason why this book is so helpful for one's spiritual life. Part of the research for the doctoral work included a qualitative analysis of the author's Dominican community. Sisters were interviewed for their insights into this prayer which is a part of their understanding of what mission means for them today. In addition, personal pastoral experiences from the author's ministry as teacher, minister, and theologian are recounted, which gives the reader a practical way of understanding and relating to the Magnificat.

The chapters include fourteen themes that flow from the song of Mary. Questions that lead to prayer, thoughts for reflection, additional scripture passages, and a personal prayer directed to God follow each theme. The reader is given a perspective that is universal, culled from the gold mine found in Luke's gospel.

Luke's beautiful portrait of Mary—upon which all sound marian theology is based—depicts her as mother, faithful disciple, a courageous woman, and a model of prayer. Mary's prayer flows from the love of the Holy Spirit within her, and she shares this gift with Elizabeth in her hymn of praise.

The fourteen themes flowing from Luke's Magnificat prepare the reader for a contemplative and joyful experience of prayer. The themes are a microcosm of Luke's theology, stressing the concepts of prayer and love for one's neighbor, which lead to a desire for world peace and justice.

The Dominicans have the motto *"contemplare et aliis tradere,"* that is, to contemplate and then share with others what has been given to them. Sister Mary Catherine has accomplished this spiritual mission of her community and challenges us to live out Mary's prayer by working for peace and justice in solidarity with God's people.

—Bertrand Buby, S.M.
Professor, International Marian Research Institute
University of Dayton

# Mary's Magnificat

## (Luke 1:46-55)

My soul magnifies the Lord,
    and my spirit rejoices in God my Savior,
For he has looked with favor on the lowliness of
      his servant girl.
    Surely, from now on all generations will call
    me blessed.
For the Mighty One has done great things for me,
    and holy is his name.
God's mercy is from generation to generation
    for those who fear him.
God has shown might with his arm;
    he has confused the arrogant in the conceit of
    their hearts.
God has pulled down the powerful from their thrones,
    and lifted up the lowly;
God has filled the hungry with good things,
    and the rich he has sent away empty.
God has come to the help of his servant Israel,
    remembering his mercy,
According to the promise he made to our ancestors,
    to Abraham and to his descendents forever.

# Introduction

## Praying the Magnificat

The Magnificat is sung or recited each evening as an integral part of vespers, the liturgical evening prayer of the church. It resounds today in churches, convents, monasteries, and other places whenever vespers is celebrated. For almost two thousand years this song has rung out in praise and gratitude to God. Over the centuries the many musical settings of the Magnificat have made this song an element of our great heritage of sacred hymns. We can join our voices today with the voice of Mary by making the Magnificat our own song.

In praying the Magnificat with Mary we are not praying alone. We pray with the countless men and women throughout the ages who have praised God in these words. As members of the communion of saints, we are part of a community that spans the centuries and today circles the globe and transcends cultures. A young Vietnamese refugee told me that since his first communion he has prayed Mary's Song as a thanksgiving after receiving the eucharist. His uncle, a priest in Vietnam, had suggested it. A Dominican sister, born and raised in a comfortable home in Chicago, remarked that she always recited the prayer silently as she returned from communion because it expressed her sentiments so well. A college professor of music traces the history of church music using the various musical settings of the Magnificat. She often sings a version of it early in the morning when she is walking her dog. "On a beautiful morning there is no better way for me to express the joy that is in my heart," she said.

An Irish missionary sister approached me with tears coursing down her cheeks after I had given a presentation on the Magnificat to tell me that she had recently been forced by war to leave the Congo after twenty years of service there. Devastated by her experiences of suffering and poverty in Africa, she found the return to her community house in California difficult. "I couldn't pray," she said. "I went for a retreat and told the director that the only prayer I was able to say was the Magnificat." She made her retreat on the Magnificat. In Latin America many of the people who are members of small base communities have made Mary's Song their own song. They see in it an expression of liberation and a proclamation of God's regard for the poor.

Praying the Magnificat with Mary assists us in entering into the interior disposition of the first and most eminent disciple of Jesus. Entering into the disposition of Mary in her prayer requires a preliminary attitude of attunement to the Spirit, a letting go of distracting anxieties. An early fourteenth-century Dominican, Meister Eckhart, defined prayer as "to stand in one's own being and to take joy in it." Feelings of guilt, doubt, unworthiness, or shame are facets of the human condition. They can separate us from taking joy in our own being. To be open to the Divine Being we need to set aside even these. Mary trusted the divine graciousness of God, and so must we. All that we fear or cringe from in ourselves can be left in her hands as we enter with her into her song, rejoicing in her joy.

Prayer is sometimes difficult when the work and distractions of everyday life leave little time for the quiet focus that reflection requires. A familiar prayer, one that has been said many times and committed to memory, can be a conduit to becoming conscious of God's presence and regard for us in the midst of our daily activities. Prayer is to the spirit as breath is to the body—a necessity of life. God loves us even when we don't pray, but when we do pray our lives change. Praying with Mary in the words of her Magnificat is a way of entering into her joy at the beginning of the Christ event.

# Background

Mary's Song, referred to as the Magnificat, is set within the context of the infancy narrative of the third gospel. The author, known to us as Luke, writes in elegant Greek to a gentile audience sometime between 80 and 85 CE. Luke probably found the song in the early Jewish-Christian community in Jerusalem. There is a strong tradition that Mary was a part of this community which was headed by James, the "brother of the Lord."

The Magnificat is a hymn very much resembling in structure the classical psalms of the canonical psalter of the Hebrew scriptures, which formed part of the traditional prayers of the people of Mary's time. The first stanza of the hymn is seen as a personal thanksgiving of Mary for the conception of her child. God is addressed as Savior, Mighty One, Holy One, One whose mercy is from generation to generation. This is the God of Israel, Mary's God. In the second stanza Mary's voice becomes the collective voice of her people, praising God who acts in history to bring all into the reign of justice, closing the gap between the powerful and powerless, the rich and the poor, the proud and the humble.

Some scholars see in the structure of the Magnificat a resemblance to hymns composed during the time of the Maccabaeans and surmise that underlying it is a victory song of late Judaism. However, the tone of the Magnificat differs from other hymns of national salvation in that there is no expression of vindictiveness. Mary does not rejoice in the defeat of Israel's enemies but in God's faithfulness to his promises. In the reign of God now breaking into human history, a situation of justice for all people will ultimately prevail because God is totally faithful to the end of all time.

A golden thread of salvation-hope runs through the poetry of the psalms as remembrance of the wondrous interventions of God in Israel's history is kept alive in songs of joy and thanksgiving. Indeed, from the Exodus to the time of the Incarnation the Lord is celebrated as the liberating and saving God by whose mighty deeds the people are delivered from slavery and the tyranny of conquerors. The joy and gladness of the poor in the salvation of the Lord is expressed in Psalms 34, 39, and 50, as well as in Isaiah 29. In her expression of gratitude and praise, Mary's voice is joined with the voices of the ancient women of Israel—Miriam, Deborah, and Judith—whose canticles ring out acclaim for God's saving deeds. The Song of Hannah, mother of the prophet Samuel (1 Sm 2:1-10), contains verses similar to those of the Magnificat in praising God's action on behalf of the lowly.

Whether or not Mary really spoke the words of the Magnificat as found in the first chapter of Luke has been the subject of scholarly discussion. Certainly the sentiments were hers. Luke puts the words of this song on the lips of Mary and includes it at the beginning of the gospel for his own theological purposes. Indeed, the Magnificat sets the themes that Luke will consequently develop in the rest of his writings, themes of messianic joy, mercy, universal salvation, regard for the poor, and prayer. The coming of the reign of God is central to Luke's theology. It forms the core of Jesus' preaching. The reign of God is present in the here and now in a mysterious way. It is wherever Jesus is present, wherever the power of God is at work bringing about the salvation of all. It will come in fullness at the end time.

The Magnificat announces the time of salvation and praises the Lord's way of acting in history to bring about the fulfillment of God's plan according to the promise given to Abraham and Sarah and their descendants. Mary is presented as the central figure at the beginning of the salvation-event. It is she who first receives the fullness of the Holy Spirit. She is the first of the disciples and is found with them at Pentecost when the whole church receives the Spirit. The joy and gratitude expressed by

Mary in the Magnificat is characteristic of the gladness that accompanies the response to an announcement of salvation in Luke's gospel.

As a prelude to the beatitudes and woes of Luke's account of Jesus' great sermon on the plain (6:17-49), the Magnificat speaks of God's regard for the poor and lowly. Mary extols God's mercy. The third gospel has been called the gospel of mercy and great pardons as well as the gospel of messianic joy. Another theme of Luke's is that of prayer. Mary says, "Holy is God's name" (1:49). Jesus teaches his disciples a prayer which begins, "Father, hallowed be your name" (11:2).

The Magnificat is set in the context of a journey. As a dynamic participant in God's plan, Mary sets off on the road to Elizabeth's home to share with her cousin the wonderful and astonishing things that God has done for her. It is reminiscent of the great journey of her people into freedom, the Exodus, which began with the wonderful and astonishing works by which God made it possible for a lowly and powerless people to escape from slavery. It was the strong hand of the Lord which led them. Mary, the lowly and powerless recipient of God's favor, praises the Lord who has shown might with his arm and who has come to the aid of his people.

In Luke's gospel we will find Jesus on a journey to Jerusalem, bringing his earthly mission to fulfillment in that city. The disciples gathered there with Mary will receive the Holy Spirit and another journey will begin as the good news moves out beyond the Jewish world into the gentile world. Luke will document the missionary journeys of Paul as he preaches the good news and brings it finally to Rome. In reflecting on the theme of journey, we might call to mind that life itself is a journey. We come forth from God and return to God, bringing with us the experiences and adventures of our itinerary.

The Magnificat opens with Mary's personal expression of gladness and rejoicing because of God's regard for her who is lowly. However, it is common in Hebrew poetry that the favor of the Lord bestowed upon an individual is considered to be for all the people. In personal prayer it is good to remember that our own blessings and gifts are given to us by God for others as well as for ourselves. In calling herself lowly, Mary places herself firmly within the community of the faithful, but poor, people of Israel spoken of by the prophet Zechariah. It is from this messianic people that salvation was to come. All that these devout ones stood for is concentrated in Mary, who forms the link between the Old and New Testaments. As the lowly servant of God, Mary is the antithesis of the arrogant whom God has confused or scattered "in the conceit of their hearts."

As a woman of Israel, Mary belonged to a people who understood themselves to be in a special relationship to the Lord, their God. This relationship, known as the covenant, was in the form of a solemn agreement whereby God promised to hold the people as his own, to care for them and save them. God's commitment to the covenant was certain and everlasting. Indeed, the justice of God lay in God's will to save. For their part the people were committed to worship only the Lord and to keep the Law. The Law required the people to treat each other with justice. The covenant was not an agreement between equals but between the all-powerful Lord, the Mighty One, and people who had both the strengths and weaknesses of human nature. The mercy of God of which Mary speaks is extended to all who fear God, that is, to all who are in right relationship with God. The mercy is God's covenant—loving kindness which is faithful from generation to generation. A social dimension is involved, for one cannot be in right relationship with God without being in right relationship with others.

In the second part of the Magnificat the three great human self-sufficiencies—pride, power, and riches—are set forth as forces opposed to God and to the people who have a special claim on God's protection, the poor and lowly. In a final great act, God is bringing about the reversal of their situation. Mary, positioned in the midst of the lowly ones, has the prophetic vision to observe the reversal of the situation of social sin, rooted in personal sin, that is brought about by the coming of the Messiah. This reversal is consistent with the way that God has dealt with his people in the past, especially in the Exodus when God thwarted the power of the Egyptians and brought the people from oppression to freedom.

In the conclusion of the Magnificat, the regard that is shown to God's servant Mary is extended to God's servant Israel, for God remembers covenant mercy. The in-breaking of the reign of God, the situation of peace, justice, and right relationships, has occurred. The time of salvation has come. Mary's Song becomes the voice of the whole church expressing joy and gladness for the great saving event.

## Thoughts for Reflection

+ Consider some way in which you feel blessed and thank God for that blessing in the words of Mary's Magnificat.

+ If a word, phrase, or idea from Mary's Song especially captures your attention, stay with that idea. Recall it to mind during the day. God may be speaking to you in that idea.

+ Recall the beatitudes of Luke (6:20-23). The beatitudes are gospel signposts in the reign of God, the reign of true happiness. Consider where you find your greatest happiness.

+ Mary's Song is set in the context of a conversation with her cousin Elizabeth. Contact a friend today and bring that person the joy of knowing that he or she is being called to mind.

+ There are many different musical settings for the Magnificat. It is a song. Sing it with Mary.

# An Attitude of Gratitude

## My soul magnifies the Lord.

When the sun rises in the morning it illuminates the dark corners and recesses of our homes. Flecks of light flicker on rippling streams and stirring tree leaves. Trees, stately, strong, enduring, cannot grow without their tiny, delicate leaves or pine needles. What is fragile may be the most important thing of all. Tiny leaves soak up sunlight. So wonderfully created, sun rays from the heavens, air, the breath of living things, and minerals and water from deep in our ancient earth are drawn together in a tiny, almost transparent leaf. Life is at work here. In an invisible explosion of activity new matter is created and nurtured.

Life is expansive. The tree is working to grow and in the process of self-growth absorbs the spent breath of other living creatures, while at the same time breathing out for them the freshness of pristine life-giving oxygen. All living things strive for growth and transformation. All are interconnected in this common endeavor. Age is irrelevant. Young and old share in the lifelong process of transformation. Those at the beginning and near the end of life are fragile, but these are the most important times of all.

There is an appointed time for everything, and a time for every affair under the sun. The early ages of life are filled with wonder and discovery. The later age of life is the time of integration. It is a time to bring together the totality of life's experiences into a dazzling unity of joy and pain, failure and success, gain and loss, giving and receiving, achievement and struggle. All comes together in gratitude, gratitude for the whole adventure of one's life.

Magnificat! Mary sings forth her gratitude to God. Gratitude is an attitude, a stance toward life. In later life, Mary surely remembered the time of gratitude at the beginning of her motherhood. An attitude of gratitude anchors us in hope that whatever suffering the circumstances of life inflict upon us, all is meaningful in God's regard for us. All has led to the present moment of our lives, and life itself is good.

The astounding courage that comes from a life lived in gratitude was brought home to me one Christmas when I drove through a near blizzard from Detroit to Chicago to visit my family and bring communion from the Christmas liturgy to my ill elderly mother. My heart ached as I entered the nursing home, and my senses were assaulted by the sights, sounds, and smells of the place. My mother's face glowed as she greeted me. My face seemed familiar, but my identity was uncertain. After receiving the eucharist with great devotion, my mother spent some time in prayer. Then, turning to me with a beautiful smile, she told me to always remember to thank God for life's blessings. "God has been so good to us," she said. "Pa used to gather us together around his chair and remind us to always remember God's goodness and be grateful." Alzheimer's disease had not obliterated the attitude of gratitude that had permeated my mother's life.

It is not what we do but who we are that is precious in God's sight. What had Mary done to be chosen as mother of the Savior, who was so young, so lowly? "What have I achieved during my lifetime?" is not the appropriate question for the later years of life. Who was Mary that she was chosen? "Who am I at this moment?"—that is the question. It is the quality of love with which we live our lives that is important.

"Hail, favored one!" the angel sang out in greeting Mary. Hail, one already transformed by God's life within. In union with her Creator, Mary became *Theotokos*, "God-bearer." Such mystery is overwhelming. Yet at the time of annunciation, Mary was transformed by the same Spirit which fell upon the disciples of Jesus at Pentecost and is today present for us. Mary was the first of many believers, first in discipleship, first in love. The great medieval preacher, Meister Eckhart, exhorted all to be "mothers of God."

Our Creator bestows life, and creativity flows from who we are. With God we continue to create life within ourselves even as our true self, our authentic person, unfolds. We can seize the moment of creativity. It is like a raft in the stream of consciousness. We can stay alert and board the raft as it passes us, or it may be far downstream before we awake.

No matter the joy or pain of present circumstances, we can reach beyond where we are at any moment and look back with gratitude to where we once were. The pain of times of darkness and struggle fade as the light of a new understanding of who we have become in God's embrace brings clarity and gratitude. The psalmist speaks of the suffering of darkness, but with the dawn rejoicing. What has been transforming for us we will remember with gratitude.

If gratitude is the attitude of a healthy spiritual life, the shadow side is resentment. Resentment is crippling. Resentment shrinks the capacity to love. Resentment is the attitude of an unhealthy spiritual life. For the converted personality, a backward glance over life's experiences is viewed with gratitude—even for the hard experiences, because they led to growth and self-knowledge. In fact, everything looks a little better than it really was. On the other hand, for the unconverted personality, a glance over life's experiences is often viewed with bitterness. Everything looks a little worse than it really was. Every effort must be made to unearth the root causes of resentment, and time must be taken to begin healing it in its early stages before it festers and grows as does a cancer, choking out the normal movement toward spiritual wholeness.

I once spent several nights in the hospital sitting beside a Sister who was in the terminal stages of cancer. In the depth of the night she would often awake and share stories of her life. She loved life and had many happy memories, but one thing troubled her. For many years she had been praying for reconciliation between her mother and her sister. The sister had married a man of whom her mother disapproved and who was of another religion. The sister was angry and hurt by her mother's rejection of her husband and severed all ties to her. Many years passed and the alienation had hardened into bitterness on both sides. Early one morning a brother of the dying sister brought her now elderly and widowed mother to visit her. Shortly after they had arrived, the door opened cautiously and the alienated sister peered into the room. Her eyes met her mother's eyes. No one spoke. There was a hush in the room. Then in a mutual movement, mother and daughter crossed the room and fell sobbing into each other's arms.

A wide chasm of pain and resentment that had kept apart two people who loved each other was bridged that morning at the bedside of a dying loved one. Mother and daughter had lost many years of knowing each other and soon were to lose the one whose illness had brought them together. But gratitude filled the room that morning.

We may think that our wounds are so deep that it is beyond our power to rid resentment from our lives. With

God though, all things are possible. There is an intercon-
nectedness to all life, and when we help each other, all of
life expands together toward union with God. We need
each other. A soul friend, a counselor, or a spiritual director may help. Mary shared her situation with the older
Elizabeth. Mary stands beside us to encourage us on our
own journey. Others may help us enter into Mary's attitude of gratitude. Pray with her the words of her
Magnificat. Healing of resentment is possible as gratitude
expands.

## Thoughts for Reflection

+ Enter today into Mary's attitude of gratitude.

+ What are the blessings in your life for which you are
  grateful? Who are the people for whose love you thank
  God? What are the events which expanded your
  understanding of yourself and of God? Is there something in the painful events for which you can find
  gratitude?

+ Are there unhealed wounds in your life that have
  caused you resentment? Is it time now to let go of that
  resentment? Do you need help from another?

+ Today is a good day to express gratitude to God and to
  others.

# Additional Scripture for Reflection

Everything growing from the earth, bless the Lord (Dn 3:76).

There is an appointed time for everything,
 and a time for every affair under the heavens (Eccl 3:1).

## Prayer

For my life and for all of creation, I give you thanks, O Lord. Thank you for all that I have learned through the events of my life, joyful and sorrowful. Heal in me the wounds that limit me from living with a healthy attitude of gratitude. Bless all those who have been good to me in any way. Bless those who have helped me grow in love. With gratitude I lift up to you all those I love and ask your blessing upon them this day.

Mary, with you I magnify the Lord. Help me to recognize the presence of God within me as Elizabeth recognized God within you. Be a healing presence for me as I go about the tasks of today.

*Joy*

# My spirit rejoices in God my Savior.

According to Luke's account, when Mary heard that her cousin Elizabeth was with child she hurried to visit her. From Mary's home in Nazareth of Galilee, which is in the north of Palestine, to the hill country of Judea in the south is not a short trip. Most likely the journey was made on foot and would have taken three days.

Today, the Church of the Visitation, built on a high hill in Ein Karem, a town not far from Jerusalem, is a memorial to Mary's encounter with Elizabeth. No road gives easy access to the shrine. The pilgrim must labor up the steep incline upon a long flight of steps. The climb is well worth the effort, for the hillside is bright with flowers and the air is pure and clear. A quiet peace pervades the site, a calm oasis in a troubled land which has so often endured the ravages of war. The name of the town itself invokes refreshment and abundance. Ein Karem means "The Vineyard Spring."

The scene of a youthful, radiant Mary being welcomed reverently and hospitably by the aged Elizabeth has been a favorite of artists over the centuries. Symbolically,

Elizabeth personifies the wisdom and holiness of all those faithful people who received God's mercy in the long tradition of the first covenant. Mary, transformed by grace, stands at the point of the in-breaking of the messianic reign of God. A new and astonishing relationship between God and humanity has been forged in Mary who bears God's Son. It is the dawn of the New Covenant.

Joy permeates the encounter. Elizabeth responds to Mary's arrival with joy and humility: "Most blessed are you among women, and blessed is the fruit of your womb. And how does this happen to me, that the mother of my Lord should come to me? For at the moment the sound of your greeting reached my ears, the infant in my womb leaped for joy" (Lk 1:42-44). In turn Mary's joy pours forth in praise of God. "My soul magnifies the Lord, and my spirit rejoices in God my savior, for he has looked with favor on the lowliness of his servant girl."

The cause of Mary's joy is God's intervention in her life and in human history. Her joy overflows in the experience of God's regard for her who is poor and of low estate. In Luke's gospel, joy accompanies announcements of salvation. Mary has called God "my savior." In Hebrew "savior" and "Jesus" are synonymous. Joy is also linked with the condition of being poor and lowly. Biblically, those whose life situation provides them with scarce resources and who experience a profound sense of their dependence have a special claim on God's beneficence. Luke's first beatitude proclaims, "Blessed are you who are poor, for the kingdom of God is yours."

The mysterious reign of God has begun. It is full of surprises. Is joy to be found in a situation of poverty and lowliness? Mary's Song is a song of the upside-down reign of God. Expectations of happiness lying in prestige, power, and wealth are frustrated. Joy is experienced in the recognition of God's dynamic presence in one's life, in the life of a community, and, more broadly, in the forces that shape human history.

When Jesus was asked where the reign of God was to be found, he responded that the reign of God is in our midst. It is in the midst of our families, our communities, our workplace, our place of worship, our place of play. Most specifically, the reign of God is in the midst of the web of relationships in which we exist. It is the reign of right relationships. It is wherever God is acting to lead individuals to holiness. It is also wherever God is acting to bring whole groups of people into a situation of justice and peace. Joy, for us, is to be part of the action.

Mary, transformed by grace, chooses to risk all to be part of the action. She recognizes that God's regard is not only for her but for all her people. She rejoices in God's action. Amazement that God should choose to share the work of salvation with a woman of such low estate pours from her humble heart.

Embarking on an arduous journey of compassion to her elderly cousin was the response of a generous heart to bring joy and assistance to another. Joy was found in the encounter at the end of a journey recorded at the beginning of the third gospel. Joy can be found in simple things: the unexpected blooming of roses in a garden, being met at the airport by a loved one, smiling at someone and receiving a smile in return. Joy may come unexpectedly like a flash of lightening in the midst of a dark storm. It may accompany a moment of insight when pieces of meaning in our lives come together. The reign of God is in the midst of joyful relationships.

Joy accompanies inner freedom. There is a deep longing in the human heart to experience the freedom which is of the essence of personhood. What limits our inner freedom? Is it fear of losing something that society tells us is important? Do we fear trying new things because, knowing our own limitations, we fear failure and looking foolish?

A certain shy and reticent college student had for months longingly gazed at a young woman who sat near him in class, but he was afraid to show interest in her. She seemed to totally ignore him. Then at Halloween there was a costume dance. Deciding to dress as a ghost, he cut eye and mouth holes in a white sheet. That night in anonymity he found the courage to ask the young woman for a dance. As the evening progressed, he became more animated, laughed, joked, and danced to his heart's content. She enjoyed his company very much but was unable to discover his identity. The next day she searched among her friends trying to discover who had so entertained her at the party. As usual, she ignored the young man seated near her who had retreated into his silent self, afraid to be discovered.

Fear to appear foolish, to lose dignity, to lose prestige, to lose power, to fail, or to be rejected limits freedom. Fear of not being good enough, not being holy enough, not being worthy even, causes us to distance ourselves from what we truly desire—to love and be loved. God regards us just as we are at this moment in time, with our strengths and weaknesses, our good deeds and our sins. God's love for us does not depend on who we are but on the fact that we are. To know who we are and to embrace who we are as loved by God is what it means to be humble. Mary knew God's regard for her. She was free to risk all for God because she could risk being regarded unfavorably by others. In her humility Mary embraced the truth of her lowliness and found joy in God's presence.

The need for security is deep in the human heart. Beyond security, desire for the status, power, and privileges associated with wealth characterizes much of the striving in modern society. In the upside-down reign of God it is a dangerous desire. Those who seek out Jesus with faith and good will find healing and joy in his presence. The sorry tale of one good young man who turned away with sadness from Jesus' invitation to discipleship because he could not part with his possessions warns us of how joy can be sacrificed to wealth.

For many people, there is something more desired than wealth, and that is *time*. Time is a precious commodity in our modern lifestyles. At a conference on world hunger, I encountered a Quaker lady who radiated joy as she told me her story of choosing simplicity of life in order to have time to follow the inclinations of her heart. She and her husband owned a small but prosperous business in a small city. One day in prayer they felt a call to become personally involved in responding to the situation of hunger which was evident in a small way in their city, in a large way in the world. The business was consuming much of their time. After much soul-searching, they sold their business. They wanted to embrace a simple, contemplative way of life where their needs would be few and they would have time for prayer and to help others. For them this meant using the few acres of land on which their home was located to raise bees as a way of supporting their family.

To their joy, persistence led to success with the bees. The carefully attended kitchen garden flourished. Extending the garden enabled them to raise an abundance of vegetables to share with the local soup kitchen. In telling her story, she emphasized over and over her delight at having time to do what she and her husband thought was important. They had time to become active in organizations that work to alleviate world hunger. The venture had begun as a risk. In it they found joy.

Overwork and anxiety mark the lives of many today who must cope with the complexities of living in a culture where wealth and privilege are admired and sought after. Expectations that others have of us may make it difficult to choose simplicity as a lifestyle. But taking even one small step on a journey to simplicity by divesting ourselves of something that we really don't need may reverse the process of being possessed by our possessions. Being attentive to what devours our time but does not bring joy may lead to insight about where we really want our energies to go.

St. Thérèse of Lisieux, recently elevated to the rank of doctor of the church, found joy in doing small things with great love. A task as tiny as picking up a piece of thread from the floor of the convent community room was for her a way of serving her sisters and loving God. She did not aspire to heroic tasks but embraced the littleness of who she was and found there a way to holiness. Joy can be found in small things. Surprising another by preparing a special celebration for a birthday or anniversary is a way to bring joy to others. Rejoicing in others' joy enhances our own.

The people of Nicaragua celebrate La Purissima, a special festival of joy on December 7, the eve of the feast of the Immaculate Conception. Many people erect small shrines for Our Lady in front of their homes. Flowers, streamers, and lights decorate the shrines. Children sing songs in honor of Mary as they process from house to house knocking on doors and asking the question, "Who causes our joy?" The homeowner responds, "La Conception de Maria." Gifts are then given out. La Purissima is also celebrated on different days within families. The entire rosary is recited, pausing after every few decades to receive juice, then fruit, and finally candy. Homemade toys are given to the children.

Mary rejoices in God's regard for her. She shares her joy with Elizabeth. Elizabeth and the child within her womb rejoice in the presence of Mary who bears the Lord. Mary's Song pours forth with joy in praise of God, both for her personal blessing and for the way God has acted on behalf of her people. Joy is in the reign of God present in our midst. "Blessed are you who are poor," Luke writes, "for the kingdom of God is yours."

# Thoughts for Reflection

+ Enter today into Mary's disposition as she sings to God. What gives her joy? When did you last experience joy? What was its cause? What does this tell you about yourself?

+ Throw a party to celebrate a special event. Share in others' joy and share your joy with others.

+ In some psalms we witness the psalmist pouring out his or her pain and sorrow to God in colorful images. After a recital of grievous suffering, the psalmist expresses confidence in God's care and turns to expressions of joy. In times of pain or sorrow, pray Psalms 30, 32, and/or 126.

At dusk weeping comes for the night;
   but at dawn there is rejoicing (Ps 30:6).

Those who sow in tears
   will reap with cries of joy (Ps 126:5).

+ Read chapters 15 and 16 of the Gospel of John. There are references there to the joy that is in store for the disciples when they receive the Holy Spirit. This is part of the great Last Supper discourse. Trust Jesus' promise to send his Spirit that our joy may be full.

# Additional Scripture for Reflection

"For at the moment the sound of your greeting reached my ears, the infant in my womb leaped for joy" (Lk 1:44).

"I have told you this so that my joy might be in you and your joy might be complete" (Jn 15:11).

## Prayer

---

I praise you, Lord, source of my being, for the gift of life and for all its blessings. Open to me the wellsprings of joy that your presence brings. May I rejoice in your Word and in your Spirit.

Mary, with you I pray, my soul magnifies the Lord, my spirit rejoices in God, my Savior, for God has regarded my lowliness and need. Walk beside me, Mary, that I might recognize God's presence in the people I encounter and see God's hand in the events of the day. Share your joy with me as you did with Elizabeth. In turn I shall share this joy with others.

# God's Regard

---

For God has looked with favor on
the lowliness of his servant girl.

---

*M*ary, a young Jewish woman, praises God in the tradition of her people. The gracious regard of God who
looks upon the lowly status of Mary is the same God of
the psalmists who looks upon the afflicted to rescue
them. Mary calls herself servant or handmaid. As a handmaid of low estate, Mary occupies a position of poverty
and powerlessness in her society.

Being lowly is not deemed to be a happy state in our
society. The lowly are often ignored. Many times they live
in loneliness and isolation. They wait in line for social
services, in medical clinics, perhaps in food lines or shel-
ters. Transportation may be problematic or nonexistent,
adequate housing uncertain. One does not aspire to be
lowly or powerless in the land of abundance. Yet, in the
beatitudes of Luke's gospel, the poor are deemed happy
because the kingdom of God is theirs. We wonder at this
word. Does a condition of lowliness give one a special
claim on God? Are the lowly more attuned to their own
need for God and more attentive to the needs of others?

We hear God's word through the ears of our own experience and we wonder.

Mary here places herself in the midst of a special group of people who have low social status, who are materially poor, powerless, and afflicted. These are the biblical *anawim*, the poor of the Lord, the faithful remnant people of Israel of whom Zechariah speaks. Mary praises God not only on her own behalf but for all these faithful, devout people. It is through them that, in the prophecy, salvation was to come to Israel. God's regard for the lowliness of Mary gives rise to the hope that God's action in casting down the mighty and raising up the lowly is now beginning; that is, the reign of God is breaking into human history.

God is personal and caring. In the biblical sense, grace and abundance result when God's benevolent face is turned toward one. Like the sun that sheds life-giving rays upon green plants, God's gaze is life-giving and empowering. As the morning sun dispels darkness and penetrates murky corners, God's gaze shines upon his loved ones, bestowing clarity of vision and insight. God's regard might also be understood in the sense of a loving parent smiling with tenderness and delight at a child. The child is powerless and knows her dependence upon the parent. Under the gaze of parental love and approval, children experience emotional security.

At the time of the angel Gabriel's visit to Mary, the Annunciation, Mary is greeted as one who is highly favored. The best known translation of the angel's greeting includes the words *full of grace*. This can also be understood as *one who has already been transformed by grace*. Mary, mother of the One who is called the holy son of God by the angel, is first recipient of the Holy Spirit which will be poured out upon the whole church at Pentecost. The well-known Christologist and Dominican theologian, Edward Schillebeeckx, explains this as follows:

The New Testament and above all the Gospel of John says that Jesus was completely filled with the Holy Spirit and acted on the basis of this gift of spiritual fullness in his earthly life. Only with Pentecost, not before, was God's Spirit, who is the Spirit of Christ, also poured out by the risen Jesus over the people redeemed by the messianic Jesus. There is one exception with regard to this pascal gift of the Spirit. The historical Miriam, Mother of Jesus of Nazareth, had already received the Holy Spirit before Easter. Mary is the first to share in the history of the Holy Spirit which takes place in our secular history, a real history set in motion by Jesus Christ, and her name is associated with his work of salvation.[1]

How wonderful to have a personal experience of God's regard, to truly know God's transforming love. Mary's privilege prepared her for her mission in life. We, too, are recipients of God's regard. The gift of the Spirit of Christ is now in the world and available to us. Faith tells us that this is so. We may believe it as we accept the truths of faith, as it is expressed in the Creed, but do we really believe it in the innermost depth of our beings?

In my association with college students I have had many conversations about faith. It seems to me that oftentimes when a young person is struggling with faith the real issue is not whether or not God exists but if God really cares. "If God exists then what does this mean for me, a less that perfect person? Can God love me, regard me with pleasure when I don't keep the rules, when I know my moral failures, my own unlovingness? I see good people suffer. How can a loving God exist?" Now most college students are smart enough to understand that it is not possible to empirically prove that God exists. Nor can it be proved that God does not exist. Neither the believer nor the unbeliever can be absolutely sure. This is the common ground between the two.

One young man sought me out after a discussion on the existence of God to tell me that he no longer believed, so he had stopped going to church. However, at the time of his confirmation he had made a commitment to the church. Now he was terrified that he was going to go to hell. This fear is not inconsistent with his statement of disbelief. It points out that deep within the human psyche there is the sense that there is someone to whom we are responsible for our actions. This sense of the *Other* may be the place where faith is rediscovered, as it was in the case of a young man who went to an isolated place, hurled a passionate statement of disbelief in God heavenward, and then sat down to wait for a response.

Suppose we risk believing that God exists, then we also risk that God may not be pleased with us. Our experience teaches us that when we measure up to others' expectations, we enjoy their approval. If we cannot measure up to what we think God expects of us, it may be hard for us to accept the fact that God loves us just as we are. "Is God pleased with me?" This is the question that underlies our spiritual anxieties. We can be told that God doesn't love us because we are good. We are good because God loves us. But unless we experience being loved by others, it is a great leap of trust to accept being loved by God.

One year I found it necessary to leave the place where I was working at the end of the first semester. I was deeply disappointed that I had not achieved what I set out to do in the situation, and although no one criticized me, I returned to the motherhouse feeling like a failure. I spent the next four months in our high school on Chicago's south side teaching mathematics. One class was made up of students who had been withdrawn from a larger math class because they were having trouble with the subject and/or were giving the teacher trouble. There were no empty classrooms, so my classes used the sewing room. At long tables and surrounded by sewing machines, I met my unsmiling and less than enthusiastic students.

They were accustomed to beginning class with a rote prayer and looked surprised when I chose to pray spontaneously. Every morning class began with a different kind of prayer—sometimes a psalm, sometimes music, sometimes silent meditation. For me it was the most important five minutes of class as I gathered my inner resources for the challenge of the rest of the hour. The students responded well and soon were taking turns offering their own prayer or hymn. The hostility to mathematics abated a bit. They brought stacks of pennies and seriously tried to grasp the concept of percentages. This was an algebra class, but there were holes in the basics. We struggled on.

Spring came late to the shores of Lake Michigan that year. Ice, snow, and overcast skies lingered beyond March and into April. One dreary afternoon I met a vendor on 71st Street who was selling daisies. I bought a large bouquet. It seemed like a hopeful sign. The next morning I distributed them to my problem students. After class one of them approached me and asked, "You like us?" "I suppose so," I responded. "How come you like us? We bad," she said, drawing out the bad for emphasis. "Well, I don't know really," I smiled, "You are obnoxious." For the first time I saw her return a smile, a bright beautiful smile. "Yeah, we obnoxious," she laughed. Then she picked up her books and left, still grinning broadly.

Of course I knew why I loved those students. It was because I identified with them in their failure. Failure had taught me empathy, and that empathy fell upon them without my even realizing it. My own limitations became a cause for gratitude for the lessons I had learned about myself.

Word came out that I wasn't going to return to the school the next year because I was to begin theological studies. A student stopped me after class and startled me by looking directly in my eyes and announcing, "I'm an atheist." I waited to hear what would come next. "But I like the way you pray," she continued. "If you come back next year to teach us, I think that I might become a believer." Was this a bribe, an offer I couldn't refuse? "Now, you know how to pray," I responded. "Even if you don't believe, you can still pray. You don't need me anymore to do that. It is my belief that whether you pray or not, believe or not, God regards you with love because deep down you are lovable." She nodded and turned away.

Mary experienced God's favor, God's loving regard of her in her lowliness. To know we are lowly, limited, sinful, obnoxious, and still loved is to experience some freedom from the underlying existential anxiety that plagues our spiritual life. "Is God pleased with me?" we wonder. We cannot know with certainty, but we can make that leap of trust in God's fidelity to us. God chose that we should be. Life is a process of understanding the truth of our own existence and of becoming what we are in God's sight—profoundly lovable.

In Mary's womb, God became incarnate in the human experience. The transforming Spirit poured out upon Mary two thousand years ago is present to us today, present in all our human experiences. God's regard for Mary in her lowliness was the cause of Mary's joy. We can rejoice in our lowliness, in the limitations of our human nature. This is where God chooses to be present. God's face is turned to us and shines upon us just as we are. Prayer may be as simple as turning our faces to God in a moment of conscious awareness that God is regarding us.

Edith Stein, a martyr of the Holocaust, was recently canonized. Born an orthodox Jew in 1891 in Breslau, Germany, she became a university teacher, philosopher, and writer. In a soul-wrenching decision and to the objections of her family that she deeply loved, Edith converted to Catholicism and entered the Carmelite Order, taking the name Sister Teresa Benedicta. Taken from her monastery by the Gestapo, she died in the gas chamber at Auschwitz on August 9, 1942. An extraordinary trust in God's love shines through her writings. This trust was a source of peace to her. She writes:

When night comes, and retrospect shows that everything was patchwork and much which one had planned is left undone, when so many things rouse shame and regret, then take all as it is, lay it in God's hands, and offer it up to him. In this way we will be able to rest in him, actually to rest, and to begin the new day like a new life.[2]

Julian of Norwich, a late fourteenth-century anchorite, had such trust in God's goodness and love for her that she puzzled over the consequences of sin. She writes that the Lord taught her that sin had no manner of substance nor particle of being. It cannot be known except by the pain that is caused thereby. "It is true that sin is the cause of all this pain. But all shall be well, and all shall be well, and all manner of things shall be well," she writes.[3]

"God has looked with favor upon the low estate of his servant girl," Mary sings out. This is the song of all who are conscious of their lowliness. Under God's gaze, all shall be well.

## Thoughts for Reflection

✦ God knows the truth of who each person is. Consider God's regard for you today as a loving glance of acceptance of who you are. In the midst of your busy day recall God's regard each time you look at a clock or watch, or pick some other way to remind yourself of it. Take a leap of trust to accept God's regard.

✦ Enter into the attitude of Mary, who accepts her lowliness, and pray with her the following verse (paraphrase of Psalm 16:5).

You, LORD, are all I have and you give me all I
   need.
My life is in your hands.

✦ Consider God's regard for those you meet or work
with today. If you are able, give them a smile,
acknowledging God's presence. It must be sincere. If
you are not able to do so because of some hurt, ask
God for healing.

✦ Take a few moments to let someone know you love
him or her. Mother Teresa of Calcutta was fond of saying that for every disease there is a medicine, except
for the disease of being unloved. The only cure for this
disease is another person who reaches out in love to
the one unloved.

## Additional Scripture for Reflection

---

"Hail, highly favored one! The Lord is with you"
(Lk 1:28).

The LORD bless you and keep you!
The LORD let his face shine upon you, and be gracious to
   you!
The LORD look upon you kindly and give you peace!
(Nm 6:24-26).

They shall call upon my name, and I will hear them.
I will say, "They are my people,"
   and they shall say, "The LORD is my God"
   (Zec 13:9).

# Prayer

God, I thank you for the love that has brought me into existence. Heal in me whatever makes it difficult for me to love others. Let me recognize the sun of your love shining upon me in every aspect of life today. Give me sharp spiritual eyes to be alert to the ways you are at work in my life. My lowliness, sin, limitations, failures, things undone, duties not attended to, people offended—all these I place in your hands. I trust your love.

Mary, you who were the first to receive the Holy Spirit at the dawn of the messianic age, pray for me and with me that I may be worthy of the favor that God bestows upon me. Walk with me in my efforts to cooperate with God's action in bringing about the fullness of God's reign where all are loved.

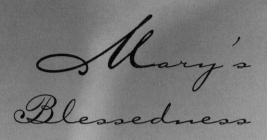

# Mary's Blessedness

Surely, from now on all generations
will call me blessed.

Elizabeth affirms Mary's condition as one who bears a holy child. The older woman shows her wise insight into Mary's inner spirit in affirming Mary's faith and trust. "Blessed are you who believed that what was spoken to you by the Lord would be fulfilled," Elizabeth states.

In her response to Elizabeth, Mary sings out with prophetic vision, "Surely, from now on all generations will call me blessed." The angel, Gabriel, tells Mary that her child will be the Son of the Most High and will reign in the House of David forever. He is to be named Jesus which, in the Hebrew form, means "Savior."

It is not unusual that a woman of Israel would claim to be blessed in the bearing of a child. Leah, the wife of Jacob, exclaimed at the birth of her son Asher, "Women call me fortunate" (Gn 30:13). Mary, however, sees beyond her personal blessing of a child to the blessing that the child will be for all people for all ages.

It is common in the psalms that the psalmist, as an individual, praises God for personal blessings but also speaks with a collective voice representing all those blessed in a similar way. The welfare of all is enhanced by the blessing given to one who has a concern for all, for the common good. Through Mary's personal blessing, the whole people are blessed. It is well to keep in mind that the talents, gifts, and blessings given to each of us are not only for us but for others. The more we share our blessing of gifts and talents with others, the more God is magnified in us. Happiness with who we are in our own giftedness glorifies God. Happiness that others are gifted in a way that we may not be also glorifies God.

Growing up in today's competitive society, we, very early, learn to compete with others for affirmation and recognition. School sports are highly competitive, as is academic achievement. Position in our workplaces may be bitterly competitive. We experience the result of the teeter-totter mentality, that for one to go up the other must go down. But sharing gifts and promoting the gifts of others puts us at least on an even keel, or at best on an elevator—everyone and everything goes up.

The great medieval cathedrals of Europe went up as cooperative ventures. There is a delightful story told of the building of the Chartre cathedral. Many tradesmen and laborers were employed in the construction, but no names of architects, masons, carpenters, or artists are known. It is recorded, however, that those rejected for work, e.g., the blind, lame, and others considered unfit for labor, seized their opportunity to get involved on a day when the regular workers were given a rest due to inclement weather. Together they hauled logs and tended fires. When the magnificent cathedral opened, it was known to be the work of the hands of both mighty and lowly, skilled and unskilled. God's house belonged to everyone.

The joy and gladness with which Mary sings God's praise for the blessing bestowed on her, a lowly one, of a holy child who will be called Savior is an echo of Isaiah's prophecy.

> Yes, the LORD shall comfort Zion . . . .
> Joy and gladness shall be found in her,
> thanksgiving and the sound of song (Is 51:3).

Isaiah is referring to the return of a poor and lowly remnant of people to their own land after a time of exile in Babylon. Zion is the place of return for the exiles. It is a hill in the area of Jerusalem, south of the temple mount, also referred to as the City of David. One of the symbolic titles given to Mary is "daughter of Zion."

The title "daughter of Zion" is a collective literary personification of the remnant people which appears in biblical literature from the time of Isaiah (after 742 BCE). More simply, it can be read *my people*. There was a notion that after the humiliation of the daughter of Zion, her glorious restoration by God would be the object of eternal admiration and blessing. The restoration of Zion is the salvific action of God in response to the prayers of the lowly in Psalm 102. In the words of the psalmist God will do this because "he has heeded the plea of the lowly, and not scorned their prayer" (Ps 102:18). The psalmist also notes that God's action will be remembered and praised by future generations (Ps 102:13-16). Mary, as daughter of Zion, reflects the communal as well as the individual recipient of God's salvific regard.

Mary states the time of her personal blessing. It is *from now on*. Luke uses this phrase several times in his gospel to refer to the coming age of salvation. For Mary, the time of which she speaks began with Elizabeth's greeting and will continue on *for all generations*. In Mary, God is beginning the final age of the exaltation of the lowly. With this in mind, we are better able to grasp the seeming paradox of the beatitudes, those signposts of the reign of God, where happiness and blessings are interchangeable:

Blessed are you who are poor;
for the kingdom of God is yours.
Blessed are you who are hungry,
for you will be satisfied.
Blessed are you who are now weeping,
for you will laugh (Lk 6:20-21).

The prayers of the lowly have always seemed to me to hold a special power. Whenever I visit someone who is homebound or in a nursing home, I ask for their prayers. More blessings have come to me from those I served than my service has ever warranted. A small example is in the following story.

One late afternoon I was waiting at the service desk of a supermarket to get a check authorized for my groceries. Ahead of me a slight, frail, elderly lady was clenching a cane in one hand and her purse in the other while a very small package was tightly held under her arm. She was pleading with the young woman at the desk for something, and the clerk was trying to be helpful. "I called the bus line company," she said. "I'm so sorry, but there is no bus going in your direction this evening." The tiny lady was not convinced. "The bus driver, who let me off, told me that he made a return trip," she insisted. The argument was going nowhere.

"Where do you live?" I asked, hoping to be helpful. "Perhaps I can take you home." The little woman spun around and eyed me, a bit suspiciously I thought, for a few moments. Then she said, "Where do you live?" When I told her that I lived across the street from the University of Dayton, she seemed relieved and then brightened up. "Well," she announced, "I live in the same direction, and I will direct you there. But if you are going to drive me home, then I will get a few more items while you shop." A mental image of this small, determined figure struggling to get on a bus with her cane, pocketbook, and small parcel flashed into my mind. Of course, she couldn't carry much.

On the drive home I learned that she was a retired schoolteacher who had never married. Having one thing in common, we talked "teacher-ese" for a while. Then suddenly she looked at me a bit slyly and said, "You're a Catholic sister, aren't you?" I admitted it. "My church means a lot to me," she said. "I always wanted to marry a minister, but it never happened. I just love the Lord."

We had crossed a river and were turning into an area of old homes when she startled me by announcing, "We are coming into my neighborhood, but you don't need to be afraid because you are with me." Being afraid had never occurred to me. In the past I had taught high school in the inner cities of Detroit and Chicago, confidently walking the streets of what some might consider frightening neighborhoods. Why would she think that I might be afraid? What was her experience? I was just a white woman driving slowly in a black neighborhood so as not to run into the children playing in the street. The children were smiling as they scattered.

When we reached her house with its steps to the long porch, I helped her up with the groceries. "Sit on the swing here while I go in," she told me. "I want to get something." "Please don't get anything for me," I said. "Let me have the blessing of doing this for the Lord." She nodded. "I would feel the same way myself," she agreed. "There is something I would appreciate," I added. "That is your prayers." She pinned me down immediately. Nothing so vague as simply "prayers" would do. She would pray for something specific, so I gave her something specific for which to pray. I was at a crossroad in my life and needed to choose a direction. She asked for a few more details about my situation and then, with conviction in her voice, informed me that I would get an answer. In a short time I had my answer.

Her message that I needn't be afraid because I was with her and to be specific about what I wanted have stayed with me and been a blessing to me. Do we expect God to give us what we want when we don't really know what we want? A restless longing in our hearts may lead us first in one direction and then another. The one sure direction is the one taken by Mary, to say to God, as she did, "I am the servant of the Lord. Let it be done to me as you say." Once we have basically oriented our lives toward God, there are still specific directions that we must choose. Once, years ago, I spoke with a young sailor who had taken a seat beside me on a train. He was not a Catholic but had seen the movie The Song of Bernadette. Being curious as to why I had chosen to enter religious life, he inquired if I had received a vision that gave me such a life direction. Remembering the long struggle that I went through in coming to this decision, I had to smile at the idea of how simple it might have been if I had be given a vision. On the other hand, perhaps I would have felt coerced and guilty if I had taken a different direction.

Freedom to choose is the essence of what it means to be human. I do not believe that we need to search for extraordinary signs or agonize too much over our choices. If we are basically oriented toward God's love, then God will be with us in whatever direction we choose after we have prayerfully and intelligently considered our options. Consulting with others known to be wise and trustworthy is always a prudent thing to do when faced with an important decision, but in the end we must bear responsibility for our own choices. When we move into the deepest part of our being and prayerfully search out that for which we most long, we come close to knowing where God is calling us. In quiet reflection we ponder the way that God is present in all the circumstances of our lives. It is here in these ordinary daily happenings that God speaks to us in the present and lights our way into the future.

The moment of Mary's acceptance of her role as Mother of the Son of God was a pivotal point in the turning of the universe. Upon her reply, a new phase of human history began. Her clear direction was to cooperate with God's plan of salvation, whatever that would mean for her. She had to face the future in faith and trust. The aged Elizabeth, with the wisdom of her years, understood the faith that was needed and affirmed Mary in her trust in the Lord's promises.

A nurse who works with psychiatric patients once remarked to me that Mary must have had a healthy self-image to be able to claim that all generations would call her blessed. The concept of a healthy self-image is a modern one. To have clarity concerning who one is and in what direction one is going is to be blessed indeed.

My work with college students has convinced me of the blessing there is in being grounded in one's life purpose. There is a basic direction in life from which all other directions flow. Thomas Merton states it succinctly when he writes about prayer:

> The gift of prayer is inseparable from another grace: that of humility, which makes us realize that the very depths of our being and life are meaningful and real only insofar as they are oriented toward God as their source and their end.[4]

The humility of which Merton speaks is knowing the truth of who we really are in the light of who God is. It was Mary's humility that gave her clarity of vision. First-year college students often arrive on campus with delightful confidence and enthusiasm. They are filled with dreams for the future. By senior year the dreams may have been altered by their experiences. Perhaps they have changed their major course of studies several times. Yet the dream is still there. These students may have no clue what life holds for them, but have a basic orientation toward God and to understand oneself as a participant in the coming of the reign of God is indeed a blessing.

Existential philosophers might characterize life as absurd, but those who share Mary's faith trust that just to be is blessing, for the ultimate goal of life's journey is union with God. Jessica Powers, in her poem "Humility," depicts the confidence that humility instills in us as we steer through sunshine and storms in life's journey toward fulfillment of God's plan for us.

Humility is to be still
under the weathers of God's will,

It is to have no hurt surprise
when morning's ruddy promise dies,

when wind and drought destroy, or sweet
spring rains apostatize in sleet,

or when the mind and month remark
a superfluity of dark.

It is to have no troubled care
for human weathers anywhere.

And yet it is to take the good
with warm hands of gratitude.

Humility is to have a place
Deep in the secret of God's face

where one can know, past all surmise,
that God's great will alone is wise,

where one is loved, where one can trust
a strength not circumscribed by dust.

It is to have a place to hide
when all is hurricane outside.[5]

One semester I had a thoughtful young man from Ghana in my class on world religions. When I asked the class what they hoped to get out of the course, Kwesi replied that he wanted to know why people who worship the same God are killing each other. It was a question to which I had no answer. At the end of the term, Kwesi told me that the class had assisted him in finding a basic direction for his life. He wanted to return to Africa as a lawyer and spend his life working for justice and peace. A few months later, I received a letter from him thanking me for helping answer his questions. He began the letter with an African proverb which reads, "It is only when a life has ended and ended well, that one dare say 'well done.'" He went on to say that before one's life can end well it must have a direction, and someone is needed to help in finding that direction. What has happened to Kwesi I don't know, but I have kept the letter as a reminder of the blessings of my own vocation.

In Mary's blessing of divine motherhood, all humanity is blest for all time. In sharing our own personal blessings, others are blest. The rest of Mary's life would be oriented toward the coming reign of God realized in her son. She kept on course in faith and trust, humility giving her the clarity of vision to see the way. Jesus' highest praise of his mother is not for her motherhood but that she is the paradigm of the disciple—one who trusts that the promises of the Lord to her will be fulfilled; one who hears the word of God and keeps it. Her trust and faith led her to the foot of the cross and to the experience of resurrection.

## Thoughts for Reflection

✦ Ponder the blessings in your life. Enter today into Mary's attitude of gratitude for these blessings. Give thanks to God.

✦ Name your blessings. Be specific. Name others through whom blessings have come to you. Ask God's blessings upon them.

- Contact someone today who has blessed your life. A brief call, a short note, or an e-mail perhaps will brighten his or her day.

- If a hurricane of life is swirling about you, find the still point, the eye of the storm, where God is present. Seek and surrender to the direction in which God seems to be leading.

- The word *humility* comes from the Latin word *humus* which means *earth*. Think of humility as the down-to-earth truth of who you are—one cherished and held in God's love.

## Additional Scripture for Reflection

"Behold, I am the handmaid of the Lord. May it be done to me according to your word" (Lk 1:38).

"Blessed are you who believed that what was spoken to you by the Lord would be fulfilled" (Lk 1:45).

"Blessed is the womb that carried you and the breasts at which you nursed." Jesus replied, "Rather, blessed are those who hear the word of God and observe it" (Lk 11:27).

## Prayer

Lord, you know me better than I know myself. I trust your love which has willed my existence. Thank you for the blessings of my life. Thank you, also, for the lessons that I have learned through painful experiences. In your love all is blessings. With a grateful heart I lift up to you all those whose lives have blessed me and ask you to give them joy in your presence, to comfort them in adversity, to surround them with love. I pray that others, especially those whom I care for the most, may find their lives blessed because of my blessedness.

Mary, woman of faith and trust, walk beside me today. Keep me on course that all I do may be done in a manner pleasing to God. You who brought the Son of God to birth, assist me to be a bearer of God fior others.

God's Wonders

---

# For the Mighty One has done great things for me.

---

Mary's praise of God continues with naming a second reason for her gratitude, the first being God's regard for her lowliness. The angel Gabriel has affirmed for her that nothing is impossible with God (Luke 1:37). Now Mary sings out her praise to the Mighty One who has done great things for her. God's might is the first of three attributes of God that Mary will praise in this verse and the next. She praises God's might, God's holiness, and God's mercy.

In the Judaism of Mary's day, there was a growing emphasis on the transcendence of God, and, out of reverence, the name of God, Yahweh, was avoided. Yet the essence of God was found in his power, and the term "Mighty One" was one of the ways by which God was named. In Psalm 89 and in the prophecy of Zephaniah this title for God denoted the power by which the warrior God saved Israel in battle.

The power of the Most High overshadows Mary in the conception of Jesus (Luke 1:35). Mary is told that her son will be the Son of the Most High and that she is to name him Jesus, which means Savior. The early Christian community held that the salvific might of God was made visible in Jesus, as is seen from the speech of Peter in Acts 2:22. It is the power of God which invests the *great things* that Mary claims God has done for her, with its meaning as *astonishing beyond understanding*.

In the Greek language of the text of the Magnificat, the word for *great things* is *megala*. It is the same word that is used to express the great and wonderful things done by God, especially in rescuing his people from Egypt and in the restoration of Jerusalem after the return from the Babylonian Exile. These *great things* are made more specific in the second half of the song where Mary speaks of God's action in confusing the arrogant, pulling down the powerful from thrones and lifting up the lowly, filling the hungry with good things and sending the rich away empty, coming to the help of his people, and keeping his promises—all of which are things that constitute the salvation-event.

Again we understand that what is done for an individual—in this case Mary—has a social function for the entire community of believers. The great things that the Almighty, with whom nothing is impossible, has done for Mary in the virginal conception of Jesus are not her privilege alone, for Mary carries in her womb the destiny of all the people of God. In the Magnificat there is a triple reference to Mary as an individual in respect to the collective Israel: the *lowliness* of Mary and the community of the *lowly* exalted by God; Mary as *handmaid* and Israel as *servant*; Mary and the ancestors of the chosen people. Thus the Magnificat takes on an ecclesial dimension. The universal tone of *all generations* calling Mary blessed puts her in relationship not only to the people of the Hebrew covenant but to the early Christian community as experienced by Luke, and indeed to the whole church.

The story of the Exodus is the account of God leading those people that he has chosen for his own out of a condition of oppression into freedom, establishing a special relationship with them under a contract known as a covenant, and forming them into a nation governed by law. This biblical story of liberation is filled with accounts of God's marvelous intervention in human affairs, and God's actions are accompanied by signs and wonders. The Almighty One of the Exodus is a God of loving kindness who protects, but is also a God to be feared.

In Mary, a poor and lowly maiden from an obscure town in Galilee, another liberation is beginning in a quiet and hidden way—an inner liberation from guilt and fear. In the child she carries, the face of God's tender love and compassion will be revealed. A way of love, reconciliation, and forgiveness will liberate from the sins of arrogance, hatred, selfishness, and greed. All social sin begins in the human heart and the greatest liberation of all lies therein.

Two thousand years have passed since Mary's Song was written. Down through the ages the Christian people have looked to Mary as one who received God's special protection and who is advocate for them in times of danger.

My heart was touched by a migrant family that I visited one summer evening. It was late August and for the parents and their six offspring it was the end of the road that season. Each year they began their journey in Texas, working their way north to a family farm in Minnesota. They were the third generation to work for the same farm family. It had been a good year for work on the land. The harvest was abundant.

The small wooden building which housed this family was unadorned and without plumbing or electricity. Two beautiful teenage daughters had brought a tub of water from an outside pump and were busy washing dishes. The father spoke of how blessed they were but explained that they would not be returning much longer. He didn't want his daughters to continue the tradition of laboring in the fields under a hot sun. I wondered about the farm family that employed them. A grain surplus had suppressed prices. It was not a good year for a small family farmer who had to sell his grain near or even below the cost of production. Looking about the bare, sparsely furnished room, I asked if there was anything I could do for them. Secretly, I offered a prayer that whatever they asked I would be capable of providing.

They had only one request: a candle for Our Lady. On the wall of the shack a tiny shrine with an image of Our Lady of Guadalupe had been nailed. Before the image, there burned a vigil light in a glass cylinder. "Wherever we go we bring Mary with us and she protects us," the father explained with reverence in his voice. "It is our last candle, and we must always have a light for Our Lady." Ah, I breathed a sign of relief. A candle was easy enough to get. But no, not just any candle, not even a blessed one would do. It had to be a special kind of candle with Our Lady's image on the glass container. The priest at the parish didn't have one. The family had so little yet all they wanted was a special candle for Our Lady in whose intercession they placed great confidence. Sad to say, although I traveled some distance searching for one, I could find no such candle in the vicinity.

Mary praises God for the wonders that God has worked on her behalf and on behalf of her people. We praise God for the wonders God worked in Mary on our behalf in the bringing about of the Incarnation of God's Word. God continues to work wonders through Mary. All people of the Americas can rejoice in the beautiful story of the appearance of Our Lady of Guadalupe to the Indian, Juan Diego, in 1531 on a small hill called Tepeyacac, near Mexico City. Dressed in native garb, Our Lady spoke to Juan in his own Mexican language, calling him "son," telling him of her love and concern for all his people, and requesting that he ask the bishop to build a church on the site where she appeared. The barrier of prejudice between Spaniard and Indian was breached by the Virgin of Guadalupe, a wonder indeed.

Catholic tradition is rich in stories of Mary's maternal protection of those who are in need, whoever they may be. In these stories, many people, considered the dregs of society, those looked down upon by others, criminals included, are recipients of her kindness. God has done marvelous things for Mary, and in turn she does marvelous things for those who invoke her. The predominant metaphor for God as Father does not form a concept of compassion in the minds of those who have had a harsh experience or perhaps no experience of being fathered. For many through the ages, Mary has reflected the maternal face of God. She can be related to without fear.

Popular medieval images of Mary, the Lady of Mercy, show her spreading her mantle of protection over various and diverse groups of people. The comforting thought seemed to be that if our sins are so great that in justice we fear we cannot enter heaven, Mary, a compassionate mother, will see to it that we get in some way. Byzantine icons of the Madonna, however, often represent Mary as presenting or pointing to her divine son. Who can be afraid of God in the form of a little child? Indeed, the Jesus we meet in the gospels reveals the compassion of God.

Popular folk stories depict Mary doing such things as holding up the feet of a thief who is being hanged until he is thought dead and cut down, whereupon he runs away free. The story of the juggler who has no other talent but brings the one thing he can do to the church to honor Our Lady has been oft told. People in the church are shocked at the juggler performing his art before the statue of Mary. Mary, however, surprises all by reaching out to the juggler with a beautiful smile. Hearts of mothers everywhere can relate to these stories, mothers who accept with love the smallest token from one of their children.

Once I visited a family who had just lost a child. The baby, scarcely a month old, was being waked in the home which was filled with the presence of the family's seven other children. The mother was gracious and calm as she led me to view the little one. Gazing on her baby with eyes full of pain she remarked, "Isn't she beautiful? God has taken her at her most innocent." The baby was indeed beautiful. Later, the mother took me aside to share something else.

"Yesterday evening I thought my heart would break at losing this child, so precious to me. My grief was so overwhelming I thought I could not endure it. I went out into our yard. The moon was shining and casting a shadow on the side of the shed there. I saw what appeared to be an image of the Madonna and Child in the pattern of the shadow. Looking at it for a moment in wonder, I thought, no, it is my imagination. If it were an image of Mary, her robe would be moving in the breeze. The branches of the tree then began to sway a little and it seemed that the robes of Our Lady in the shadow were moving. An immense peace came over me, and I knew that my child was with God and I could bear this pain. Others may think I was imagining this, but I think Mary was comforting me."

The wonderful thing the Mighty One has done for Mary is to give her the child in whom a new covenant is established with God. In this covenant God is fulfilling the promise of the first covenant. The Lord God of Israel is leading a people, rid of fear, out of darkness and the shadow of death into the way of peace (Canticle of Zachary, Lk 1:68-79). The signs and wonders worked by Jesus reveal the compassionate One who invites us to transform our hearts and bestow on others the same love and forgiveness which has been bestowed on us.

The great fourteenth-century Dominican preacher and mystic Meister Eckhart taught that we must all be bearers of God. The same grace that was in Mary is in each of us, according to Eckhart, who exhorted his listeners to all be mothers of God. In this way, like Mary, we bear Christ to the world.

Some years ago I visited the cathedral city of Esteli in Nicaragua. The people had suffered much under the repressive dictator, Somoza. At the time of my visit, they continued to suffer from attacks by the Contras. Just before I arrived the city's electrical system had been bombed. Pumps were not working, and there was no fresh water in the city. In the small park of the plaza before the cathedral, a cross had been erected in memory of a group of teenage boys who had been cruelly killed there by Somoza's national guard. On the cross were the imprint of hands with an inscription that read, "I have no hands but yours."

We are the ones who today must bear Christ to the world. The Mighty One who worked wondrous deeds in Mary is with us in this work no matter our limitations. Nothing is impossible with God. Others may not recognize our small deeds of kindness. But remember, the marvelous work God accomplished in Mary was, for a long time, hidden.

## Thoughts for Reflection

+ Today reflect upon the presence of Christ dwelling within you. Welcome that presence and be conscious of bearing it to others.

+ Freedom is of the essence of what it means to be human. God worked marvels to lead his people out of an oppressive social situation in Egypt. In Mary, the Mighty One works marvels to bring forth a new situation of liberation—liberation from all that oppresses. Reflect on the meaning of inner freedom. What compulsions or fears limit your choices to use your gifts and talents for others? Embrace the negative aspects of yourself, knowing that the Mighty One is not limited by your limitations but needs only your good will to work marvels in you. Take a risk.

✦ In the child in Mary's womb, the reign of God was breaking into human history in a new and dynamic way. Begin reading the gospel of Luke from beginning to end in order to better understand the reign of God which Jesus preached.

✦ Consider becoming part of a group that works for a more just society. Amnesty International works for the liberation of those unjustly imprisoned. Write a letter on behalf of a prisoner of conscience.

✦ The 3.9 billion people on planet Earth are all children of God. Rejoice in the diversity among peoples and reach out in friendship to those of a difference race or culture. Support causes of justice for all peoples.

## Additional Scripture for Reflection

The LORD, your God, is in your midst,
   a mighty savior (Zep 3:17).

Mighty LORD, your loyalty is always present (Ps 89:9).

With your own eyes you have seen all these great deeds that the LORD has done (Dt 11:7).

Jesus the Nazorean was a man commended to you by God with mighty deeds, wonders, and signs . . . (Acts 2:22).

# Prayer

O God, I thank you today for the wondrous works that you have accomplished in Mary and in all the saints. Thank you also for the gifts and talents that you have given me. Be present in me as I go about my work today. Be in all those I encounter. Let me be your eyes and ears today as I see or listen to others. I pledge to you the work of my hands. May it be your work. I reject any injustice of which I have been a part in the past and ask for your Spirit to assist me in making just choices in the future.

Mary, Mother of Mercy, in your expansive vision of history you recognized how the Mighty One was at work to reconcile all people. Pray for me that I may be faithful to the use of my gifts and talents to bring God's love to others. Pray for me that I may understand how best to be part of fostering peace and justice in my own situation and in society. I pray for a loving heart and a wise mind.

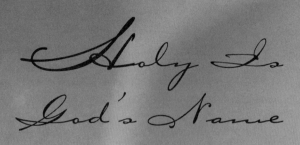

# Holy Is God's Name

---

## And holy is God's name.

---

In keeping with the practice in late Judaism, Mary does not speak God's name directly in her song. In place of God's name, Yahweh, God is called Lord, Savior, and Holy One. Elsewhere in the infancy narrative, Luke applies these same names to Mary's son. Jesus is called "Holy One" by the angel Gabriel at the time of the Annunciation (1:35), "Lord" by Elizabeth as she greets Mary (1:43), and "Savior" by the angel who announces the birth of Jesus to the shepherds (2:11). The name, person, and work of God are inseparably linked with the name, person, and work of Jesus. The infancy narrative, of which the Magnificat is a part, is contained in the first two chapters of the third gospel. In order to understand any one piece of the narrative, it is necessary to read the whole story.

The holiness of God is frequently mentioned in the Hebrew scriptures, and there are many references to the holy name of God. *Holy* expresses the transcendence of God. God is wholly apart, wholly other. Jewish law prohibited the making of any image of God because no image could represent the One who was outside and above all nature. Yet the all holy God is present to the people. The temple of God was considered holy because God's presence was there to receive the prayers and sacrifices of the people. The prophet Isaiah records God claiming to be high and exalted, living eternally, and whose name is the Holy One. This same God claims to dwell on high, in holiness, and yet also with the crushed and dejected in spirit, "to revive the spirits of the dejected, to revive the hearts of the crushed" (Is 57:15). Mary, who positions herself among the lowly ones, experiences God's holiness. The Holy One dwells with and within her.

In the Acts of the Apostles, Luke's second volume, the crucified and risen Jesus is recognized by the earliest Christians as the embodiment of God's holiness (Acts 3:14). St. Paul recognizes holiness in those who have received the Holy Spirit when he writes "the temple of God, which you are, is holy" (1 Cor 3:17). God dwells within each of us. God's holy presence is within me and within you. Catholics acknowledge this indwelling when making the sign of the cross on themselves and invoking the Trinity—Father, Son, and Holy Spirit.

What are we saying when we refer to God as holy? The words we use to speak of God have meaning for us because they come from our own human experience. We experience goodness in people and in things and so are able to comprehend the idea of goodness, and by analogy consider absolute goodness in God. The term *holy* is commonly used of persons who reflect moral goodness, great love, and total commitment to God. Thus saints are deemed holy. Also considered holy are things set apart for worshiping God. God, however, abides in mystery beyond that which our minds can comprehend. God, the Holy One, is other. An experience of the otherness of God is an experience of God's holiness.

What is this otherness as it relates to God? God is. We are not. God creates. We are created. God is creator. We are creature. Upon this truth hangs the mystery of our own existence, dependent and limited. God is holy. We claim holiness only inasmuch as God has chosen to abide with us and within us. Saints understood this truth. Catherine of Siena, anchored in self-understanding of her own dependent existence, relates God's word to her, "I am One who is. You are she who is not. You have become someone because I loved you."[6]

In stories of scripture the mysterious presence of God elicits awe and wonder. Anyone who has seen the movie classic *The Ten Commandments* will remember the scene in which Moses (Charleton Heston) encounters God on Mount Sinai. The awesomeness of God's presence is imaginatively depicted with smoke, thunder, and lightening (Ex 19:16-19). In contrast, we read that the prophet Elijah encountered God not in strong wind, earthquake, or fire, but in a tiny whispering sound (1 Kgs 19:11-12). Both Moses and Elijah are directed by God to journey to a sacred place. There they must wait for God to initiate the encounter, for God is not subject to human control.

God is experienced as holy, that is, as something beyond ordinary human experience, in an encounter which may first inspire wonder or dread but be followed by a gentle stirring in the depths of the spirit. Authentic encounter with God may initially engender fear but results ultimately in joy. The first message of the angel to Mary, after she had been greeted, was to not be afraid. God's presence is awesome, but there is no need to cower before God's holiness. One cowers before a tyrant, not before the God of compassion. The Holy One which Mary bears in her womb is the embodiment of the compassion of God. Elizabeth and her child recognize this holy presence within Mary. They are filled with joy.

As we ponder the meaning of this, we may find ourselves trying to know the unknowable and in the paradox of attempting to find words to explain what we really don't know. A friend of mine once remarked, "If we think we know who God is, we are probably mistaken." Thomas Merton, able to express himself wonderfully in words, wrote poetically of those who experience God and try to speak of it, describing them as "blind lions searching for springs in the desert." The best way to get some human understanding of an encounter with the holiness of God is from human experience. There are voices within us and outside us which speak to this experience.

Some accounts of experiencing God's presence are intensely soul-shaking; others are expressed as a gentle stirring deep in the heart. A high school senior attended a student prayer session one evening, not because he was interested in praying, but because he was interested in one of the girls who was there. The scripture reading that night told the story of Jesus washing the feet of his disciples. During the reading this young man became very quiet and withdrawn. When the meeting ended he had to be nudged into awareness that others had left the building. He gazed at me with wonder in his eyes and kept saying over and over, "Imagine having your feet washed by the Son of God."

Later, he explained that he had felt uneasy about being at the prayer service and not really wanting to pray. Then, as the scripture was being read, he had suddenly awakened to the meaning of a story he had been told before but never really heard. Peace had come over him, and a profound sense of God's love had seized him. It was a sobering event that stayed with him and caused a shift in his perception of life.

A priest once shared that he was disturbed by the fact that he had lost his faith. This terrified him. So he went to a monastery hoping that, surrounded by the faith of the monks, he would regain what he had lost. After a time he realized it was useless. He felt he needed to admit to himself that he did not believe and come to terms with this fact. Alone, in the darkness and silence of his austere monastic cell, he stood upright and shouted aloud, "God, I do not believe in you." He then sat and waited. There was no flash of lightening, earthquake, or thunder, just the dark, the silence, and the terrible aloneness. Finally, a question surfaced lightly within his consciousness. "What are you waiting for?" He laughed, knowing that he was awaiting a reply from the Other.

Jesus promised to send his Spirit to those of us who are his disciples. It is this presence of the Holy One within us that makes us holy. There is something irresistible about holiness in others. The peace and love which flows from authentically holy persons is healing for others. Burdens of guilt, fear, and self-loathing were lifted from those who encountered Jesus. Disciples of Jesus, who, like Mary, bear the presence of the Holy One to others, are often persons whose presence is healing. There is a story that the Franciscans tell about St. Clare. It seems that there was a companion of St. Francis who came down with a dreadful case of the uneasies. Francis, not knowing what to do with this anxious and fearful brother, sent him to Clare. Clare told the brother to sleep in the place where she was praying. He did this. Clare continued her prayers. Some hours later the brother arose from deep slumber with a sense of wholeness and peace, cured of his uneasiness.

There are ways to recognize holiness in others and to discern what is truly of God in spiritual experiences. One effect of the presence of the Holy One in a person's life is a genuine humility of heart. An experience of God's holiness and love leads us to see ourselves more clearly. In the light of who God is we see who we are, and this is humbling. Harsh judgement, prejudice, and intolerance of others diminishes as we comprehend our own limitedness and failure to love as God loves. Others appear more beautiful and lovable to us. St. Catherine of Siena uses the image of a mirror to explain this. "As we gaze into the mirror of God's holiness we see the spots on our own faces." Humility of heart makes us loving and lovable.

A second effect of the presence of the Holy One in our lives is poverty of spirit. There is a yearning for God that eclipses the desire for material goods, position, power, prestige, and comfort. The need to place our security in power and wealth is replaced by finding our security in God's love. There is no need to control others or use them for self-gratification. Poverty of spirit makes us trustworthy. The good of others is as desirable as our own. Those best able to be peacemakers and reconcilers are those poor in spirit. They have no turf to protect, no position to defend, no burden of hatred or passion for revenge. Peacemakers seek not control but conversion. They do not coerce but convince. They recognize and speak truth.

A third effect of the presence of the Holy One in our lives is what is called long-suffering, or patience, by St. Paul when he lists the fruits of the Spirit (Gal 5:22). This is also translated as "patient endurance." It is a determination to stay the course in fidelity to God over the long haul. It is the ability to make a commitment and remain with that commitment through many difficulties. It is the courage to remain faithful to prayer in times of spiritual aridity, the will to love in the face of hatred and injustice, the energy to strive for reconciliation in the midst of conflict. To endure suffering in order to achieve a higher good requires spiritual stamina. Dorothy Day reminded us that while love in the abstract may be romantic, love in action is "a harsh and dreadful reality."

It is wise to cast our lot with those who are able to assist and encourage us in our journey to ultimate union with God. Looking for evidence of qualities of humility of heart, poverty of spirit, and patient endurance in spiritual leaders is one way to discern where the Holy Spirit is truly at work, remembering always that even the best leader is also human and limited.

Mary proclaims in her Magnificat that God's name is holy. She has encountered the Holy One, and within her womb the Holy One has become incarnate. Mary calls herself lowly. She places herself among the poor and humble people of Israel and responds in wonder to God's regard for her lowliness. Mary is faithful to the end. She endures the pain of her son's suffering and death. After the resurrection and ascension of Jesus, she is present with the other disciples in the upper room awaiting the descent of the Holy Spirit. For generation upon generation she has been loved and trusted by those who invoke her help. Poverty of spirit, humility of heart, and patient endurance characterized Mary's life. In this she is the exemplar of one in whom the Spirit of God dwells.

## Thoughts for Reflection

+ God's presence abides within each of us no matter how unworthy we may feel. Recall to consciousness that you are a temple of the Holy One by God's choice, not by your own merit. Sit quietly for a while with this presence.

+ In dealing with others today, silently acknowledge God's presence within them. Be generous with smiles when they are appropriate. Mary bore the presence of the Holy One to others. Be conscious that you, too, are bearing the presence of Christ to others.

+ Pray the Lord's Prayer, slowly reflecting upon the phrase "hallowed be your name."

+ At the end of the day, reflect on the way that God has been present in each situation in which you found yourself. Rejoice in the good that you accomplished. Place hurts, disappointments, failures, or unfinished business in God's hands.

+ True humility accepts being loved by God for who we are in spite of all our faults and regardless of everything we may dislike about ourselves. Trust God's love that has called you into personhood.

# Additional Scripture for Reflection

When you pray, say: "Father, hallowed be your name" (Lk 11:2).

Holy and awesome is God's name (Ps 111:9).

Bless the LORD, my soul;
   all my being, bless his holy name! (Ps 103:1).

For thus says he who is high and exalted,
   living eternally, whose name is Holy One:
On high I dwell, and in holiness (Is 57:15).

# Prayer

God, hallowed is your name. I thank you for my existence. Let me continue to be conscious of your love for me. In times of darkness and doubt, remind me of your presence. My life is in your hands. I place in your hands all those I love, trusting your love for them also. Forgive my failures to love others. Heal in me the wounds of unloving words or actions that I have endured. Heal others of wounds that I may have inflicted upon them. Give me a heart to pursue reconciliation and peace with all.

Mary, filled with grace, Mother of the Holy One, pray for me. You radiated God's presence in your humility of heart, poverty of spirit, and patient endurance. Be my guide in reflecting God's presence in the world by my words and deeds. Spread the mantle of your protection over all those I love.

# God's Mercy

---

## God's mercy is from generation to generation for those who fear him.

---

*W*hen Mary sings out, "God's mercy is from generation to generation for those who fear him," a traditional understanding of the relationship between her people—the people of Israel—and God is expressed. The word *mercy* or, in Hebrew, *hesed*, denotes both a disposition and an appropriate way of acting between two parties pledged to each other in mutual trust and faithfulness. God's *hesed* means his loving kindness and faithful help based upon the covenant relationship. Those who will benefit from God's mercy are those who fear him, that is, those who have a religious and filial attitude of respect for God. In Wisdom literature of the Bible, *fear of the Lord* is equated with knowledge and insight (Prv 1:29; 2:5). Collectively, the fearing ones are the righteous ones. Righteous ones who have kept their obligations under the covenant can appeal to God's mercy with confidence. Mary has been told that her child's reign would last forever (Lk 1:33). The new covenant in Jesus is an example of God's mercy lasting from generation to generation.

When we ask God for mercy we appeal to the special bond that has been established in baptism between ourselves and God. We are not begging to be saved from the wrath of a tyrant who is about to punish us, but rather, we appeal to a loving Father who desires our wholeness and inner freedom. Justice or righteousness on the part of God is his will to save in keeping with his promise. It is consistent with God's fidelity to the covenant that his mercy endures forever. Righteousness on our part is in keeping the commandments which spell out the obligations that we owe to God and to each other.

In the gospel of Luke a lawyer asks Jesus what he must do to gain eternal life. Jesus, the perfect teacher, turns the question back to the man by asking what is written in the law about this. The lawyer, clever as he is, answers correctly and Jesus affirms him. Jesus does not need to answer the question because the inquirer already knows the answer. He must love God with all his heart, with all his soul, with all his mind, with all his strength, and love his neighbor as himself.

The startling lesson that comes next expands the concept of neighbor beyond its common meaning. In the parable of the Good Samaritan, Jesus teaches that love of neighbor shatters the boundaries of religious affiliation, ethnic identity, economic class, political ideology, race, and all else by which we exclude others from our circle of intimacy and concern. Indeed, when we pray the Lord's Prayer we ask God to "forgive us our trespasses as we forgive those who trespass against us." In other words, we plea that God will hold nothing against us, for we hold nothing against others. The conditionality of this petition may cause a tweak of fear in our consciences. The expansiveness of our own love and forgiveness can never match the gratuitousness of God's mercy, and we know it.

"The fear of the LORD is the beginning of wisdom," the psalmist writes (Ps 111:10). Biblically, *fear of the Lord* means to be in right covenant relationship to God. It is the first of the seven gifts of the Holy Spirit. From *fear of the Lord,* one grows into *reverence, knowledge, courage, counsel, understanding,* and *wisdom.* Wisdom enables one to see the divine truth in all things, to perceive how all relates to God, to realize the expansiveness of God's mercy. I have known people of wisdom and marveled at their inner freedom, simplicity, and sense of humor. When all is perceived in the light of God's loving mercy, the existential anxiety which drives much of the frantic activity seen in today's society abates. Energies are directed toward what is deemed important in God's eyes. John of the Cross, the great Carmelite mystic, states what is important: "In the evening of life we shall be judged on love."

Those who fear the Lord depend upon God's loving kindness. Yearning to experience God's mercy increases as one grows in relationship with God, passing from fear of the Lord to wisdom. The more we grow in relationship to God the more we recognize our limitations and our needs. Catherine of Siena holds a mirror before us to express this experience. Gazing into the mirror of God's perfection, we see the spots on our own faces, she writes. The more clearly we comprehend God, the more clearly we see ourselves. Mercy, God's loving kindness, is like a cord binding us to our God. As we purposely set out to live the gospel, we recognize more and more the heaviness of the load of frailty which we carry. More and more we cry out for God's mercy to hold that load for us.

Consideration of God's mercy sustains hope that God, who is absolutely faithful to his promises, is acting in the events of our lives and in the events of history. Some of these events are dark indeed. We read the words of the elderly rabbi in Elie Wiesel's story *Night* crying out in anguish in the midst of Nazi death camp prisoners, "Where is the divine mercy?" And finally, "Where is God?" Where is the mercy of God? Where is the God of mercy? For those hanging between hope and despair, the questions burn with intensity. In the six decades since the experience of the Holocaust, Elie Weisel has riveted the attention of countless young people on the deepest questions of human existence and on the responsibility to be agents of God's mercy toward all others. That the lesson has been taken is evidenced in the efforts of many to stop the horrors of genocide and ethnic cleansing, to bring aid and comfort to the victims of hatred. That the lesson has still not been taken by everyone is evidenced in the fact that genocide continues in the world today.

In the Middle Ages, images of Mary, Mother of Mercy, were carved or painted showing Mary with an open mantle under which were gathered those who honored her. The images are numerous in Europe, and the identity of the group portrayed beneath her mantle varies. Different stories interpret the image. Basically, the message is that those who suffer the anxiety of being unworthy of God's mercy may find it in the mediation and embrace of Mary. A Dominican version of the story relates that Dominic looked about heaven and failed to find any of his followers there. When he brought his concern to Mary, she opened her cloak and under it were found those he was seeking.

Another charming story of Mary's intercession coming from the Middle Ages tells of a thief who is about to be hanged for his crimes. In spite of his ungodly way of life, the thief has been in the habit of seeking Mary's intercession. As he is being led to the gallows, he once again invokes her help, beseeching her to pray that God will have mercy upon him. The execution proceeds, and the thief is left to die. To the great surprise of those who later come to cut him down from the gallows, he is found to be alive and well. A witness exclaims that the thief could not fall because a beautiful lady standing beneath the gallows held up his feet. As the sentence had been duly carried out, the thief, saved by Our Lady, was allowed to go free.

As these colorful medieval legends remind us, in all generations people of faith have recognized the need for God's mercy. People have regarded Mary, who proclaimed God's mercy, to be the very face of God's mercy, of God's absolutely faithful, loving kindness. As the Magnificat is sung or recited each evening in vespers, we hear Mary's voice proclaiming God's mercy anew to each generation.

"God's mercy is from generation to generation," Mary sings out. Two millennia after those words were written, those who fear God still find God's mercy in the events of their own lives and in history. This concept of God's faithfulness in bestowing mercy was captured wonderfully by Francis Thompson in his poem "The Hound of Heaven." God pursues the soul who tries to flee. That God's mercy spans the generations almost gives us the idea that it is inherited. Many pastoral ministers can tell stories of young people who came to them seeking to learn about a faith which they knew was that of their ancestors and which they hoped to reclaim. One young man who shared with me an account of his conversion, in which he was seized by an overwhelming experience of God's love for him, struggled with a sense of being unworthy of this love. Why was he so graced? At last he blurted out, "Well, my grandmother prays for me a lot."

Mary's faith is the faith of Israel. She announces that God is fulfilling his promise to her ancestors, to Abraham and to all the inheritors of Abraham's faith. Our ancestors in the faith have bestowed upon us a rich legacy. We belong to the communion of saints, a vast witness of believers who preceded us and now, in union with God, hold us in the embrace of love and prayer. Perhaps God's mercy is mediated to us more than we know.

# Thoughts for Reflection

✦ There is a little Russian classic of spirituality called *The Way of a Pilgrim.* Although the name of the Russian monk who wrote it is not known, the constant prayer of the pilgrim is well known: "Jesus, Son of God, Savior, have mercy on me." Today in the midst of your many activities, breathe in God's love and breathe out this prayer.

✦ Slowly pray the Lord's Prayer dwelling on the words, "Forgive us our trespasses as we forgive those who trespass against us." Ask for the grace of reconciliation and forgiveness for anyone you know who is in conflict with another.

✦ Reflect upon the faith of your parents, grandparents, or others who have mediated faith to you. Thank God for them and pray for them.

✦ Smile upon a child today. Reflect upon the way that God's love is mediated to children by those who are significant in their lives.

✦ Take a few quiet moments to be aware of God's presence and consciously accept God's love.

✦ Ponder the words of John of the Cross: "In the evening of life we will be judged on love." Consider which activities you are engaged in that are the most important in view of your final end: transforming union with God.

## Additional Scripture for Reflection

But the LORD's kindness is forever,
    toward the faithful from age to age (Ps 103:17).

Therefore, if you hearken to my voice and keep my covenant, you shall be my special possession, dearer to me than all other people, though all the earth is mine (Ex 19:5).

I will bestow mercy down to the thousandth generation, on the children of those who love me and keep my commandments (Ex 20:6).

Praise the LORD, who is so good;
  God's love endures forever (Ps 136:1).

## Prayer

Your mercy and your loving kindness are from generation to generation, O Lord. Look upon those today who are in greatest need of your mercy. Be present especially to those who suffer violence and injustice. Send your Holy Spirit to teach me how to be merciful as you are merciful. Comfort refugees and those who have lost their homes because of war or natural disaster. Open hearts to compassion for all who suffer. Have mercy on me according to the greatness of your mercy, and bring me into right relationship with you.

Mary, Mother of Mercy, for generations you have come to the aid of those who invoked you. Watch over me and all those I love. Mother of those who suffer the violence of war, pray for us. Mother of refugees and exiles, pray for us. Mother of those who fear, pray for us. Mother of Jesus, pray for us.

# God's Mighty Arm

---

## God has shown might with his arm.

---

The faith of Mary in God, her Savior, and her response to the great things that God has done for her are expressed in the first part of the Magnificat. In the second part we see that Mary's faith is the faith of Israel. The canticle that Luke puts upon the lips of Mary is sung not only for herself, as an individual, but for all the messianic people who yearn and hope for the promises of the Lord to be fulfilled. The South American women theologians Ivone Gebara and Maria Clara Bingemer speak of Mary as "Mother of the poor." In her song, Mary sings of the wonders God has done for a people, poor, humble, and powerless in the history of salvation. The same God who formed the Messiah in Mary's womb is the God who made possible the Exodus from Egypt. For Yahweh, God of Israel, nothing is impossible (Lk 1:37). Jesus, the son that Mary carries in her womb, will preach the coming of the reign of God. This reign of God happens wherever God is acting to bring about a situation of justice, peace, and love among people.

The image of God's arm appears in Hebrew scriptures to signify the miraculous demonstration of the power of God. In the Exodus, an oppressed people were brought out of Egypt by God with "strong hand and outstretched arm" (Dt 4:34). In the Book of Isaiah, the image relates to the bringing of salvation. The arm of God would show its power in fulfilling the ancient promise of a messiah. For the earliest Christians, the redemption in Jesus Christ was the supreme manifestation of the strength of God's arm.

The mighty arm of God is a military image. It is the strong arm of the warrior that wields the sword or draws the bow. This image may pale in the face of modern warfare, where it takes very little physical strength to pull the trigger of a gun or to push the button that launches a missile. Yet, it is the intent of the warrior that decides how this strength is to be used, decides the target, and determines the most opportune time to use the force which is available to him or her.

We dwell in the protective shadow of the strong arm and outstretched hand of God. "Do not be afraid for I am with you," God tells us. Mary invokes this image of the warrior God who has called her, a lowly handmaid, to be part of the unfolding plan of salvation for all people. She trusts that she is dwelling under the compassionate protection of the Most High as she moves forward in her mission to bear the Messiah—an awesome calling indeed, one that will require courage and commitment on her part. Remembrance of God's mighty deeds on behalf of her people in the past reveals the intention of the Mighty One to come to the aid of all who call out for deliverance from oppression.

The mighty arm of God, a metaphor for God's absolute power over all things, is not only for us individually but for all of us in common. In the core of the Magnificat, we hear that the strength and power of God brings about a leveling of the human condition. God pulls down tyrants from their seats of power and lifts up lowly ones. God fills the hungry with good things and sends away empty those already filled, the rich. In some sense, for some people, the image of God's almighty arm might be a frightening one; for others it is a comfort. What is it that we look to the mighty arm of God to do for us? In what and from what do we seek God's protection? For each of us it is different, for individually we have different needs, interests, responsibilities. Yet we might ask, also, what we desire the mighty arm of God's omnipotence to effect in our society.

Tales of violence against those with limited power reach us daily in news reports. Perhaps the experience of violence has touched us or someone close to us. We are afraid and respond by placing more locks on our doors and police on our streets, seeking to keep ourselves and our loved ones safe. The great danger is that retaliating to injury or injustice in a violent way escalates violence. A growing spiral of violence is difficult to stop. The gospel warns against taking revenge on enemies. Jesus teaches that we must love our enemies and pray for those who harm us—a hard teaching indeed. The example of Jesus, who suffered violence by living what he taught, is before us each time we glance at a crucifix. He is the message of God's compassion for us, calling us to love others because God has first loved us; yet, Jesus confronted evil and overcame violence with love.

Tales of heroes of faith who confront and overcome evil with good are also part of our experience. Men and women such as Dorothy Day, Martin Luther King, Jr., and Oscar Romero have confronted the forces of violence and evil, not by more violence, but by the God-given power of love and the might of solidarity with others in action for justice. Mother Teresa risked trusting in God's protection when she left the safety of her convent and ventured alone into the crowded and noisy streets of Calcutta to assist the poorest of the poor. She brought the presence of God shining within her to those abandoned and dying.

Her actions spoke her convictions that the least among us is precious in God's sight.

An image of Mother Teresa walking in the middle of a street in Beirut carrying a child remains in my memory. It was flashed on the evening news during the civil war in Lebanon. Armed men on all sides of the conflict held their fire as she evacuated children from a hospital in the war zone. Her only reported comment on the devastation she was witnessing was, "Madness." The might of God's arm aided her and the children that day.

A man of faith, Cesar Chavez was able to arouse the awareness of a nation to the plight of migrant farm workers by engaging in a well-publicized personal fast. Consciences were touched when he begged his followers not to retaliate in a violent and destructive way against the violence and injustice of those who opposed them in their efforts to bring more just working conditions. Trust in God's protection has enabled many lesser known and unsung heroes to act, not with recklessness but with courage forged by love, to walk into dangerous situations and confront evil in a non-violent manner. The age of martyrs has not passed.

In quiet moments of prayer we sit in God's presence. The face of God shines upon us. The power of God awaits our request. In our outer world there are concerns we pray about, things for which we plan, future things. But we do not live in the future, only in the now, the present moment. Face to face with God's absolute power over all things, pondering God's will to act to bring about the fullness of the reign of justice with love, we may find ourselves trembling in our shoes. The words of the Magnificat depict the mighty arm of God turning upside down the human experience of power and privilege. Ask yourself, "What is it today that I wish the power of God to do for me? Is what I ask in keeping with God's salvific plan to bring all persons into the 'reign'?" God is in the midst of our world acting to order all things for our good. God is also present to us in our inner worlds.

With what do you wrestle in your inner world? What is it there that you wish the mighty arm of God to do for you? In the quiet of God's presence, under God's gaze, we can see ourselves as limited and imperfect. In the silence and solitude of prayer, monsters within may raise their ugly heads. In the busyness of the work-a-day world, their presence may not be evident, but they tend to surface in times of quiet and aloneness. What are these monsters? They may be feelings of guilt, fear, depression, anxiety, abandonment, inadequacy, etc. You name them for yourself. We try to keep them under control or get rid of them all together, but they seem to keep returning.

We are children of original sin, and we all share the human condition. Everyone to some extent has been battered and bruised by the condition of sin, the lovelessness that exists in our world, in our society. If only an inner hero would slay the monsters and set us free from this threat of inner pain and chaos. There is hope! "God has shown might with his arm." God wields absolute power over all things. In the blazing light of God's passionate love for us, monsters of darkness have no more power than we choose to give them. Do not be afraid to gaze at God, even with your imperfections. The monsters within are known to God. Remember, God chose to take on the human condition and God loves us just as we are, monsters and all. We are all loved even with spots on our faces.

God, of course, could slay our monsters, but our God, the Holy One, is Yahweh, the God of life not death. Whatever monsters dwell within us, whatever sins, limitations, or obnoxious aspects of our personalities, these do not limit God's love for us. All fall under the absolute power of God's mighty arm. Before God's gaze we can stand erect and lift up our heads, knowing we are secure in God's love, power, and protection. God's strong arm defends our inner selves. As for the monsters, make them your pets, tame them, embrace them, give them a pat, and send them to sleep. Leave them in the shadow of God's strong arm and outstretched hand. Let no energy be sapped trying to control them. Enjoy your inner freedom and use your energy for love and service. In this way the reign of God is furthered.

There is a place where our inner lives flow into our outer lives. This is the place where God is inviting us to be part of the mission of Jesus, to put our gifts, talents, and energy to furthering the reign of God. In the Lord's Prayer we pray, "Your kingdom come." To cooperate with God in bringing about a more just and loving society is what we are about when we pray this prayer. There is no time to cower before monsters. We need all our inner resources to operate effectively in the outer world where we find our mission. Mary proclaims that God has shown might with his arm. God, who liberated the Israelites from Egypt, continues to lead to freedom those in right relationship with God and with each other.

"Your will be done," we pray. Where is God's will to be found? God is present in the midst of our activities and speaks to us in the quiet core of our spirits. Mary trusted that God would continue to fulfill the promises made to her ancestors. Let us trust the might of God's strong arm stretched over us to cherish, protect, and point the way to the future.

## Thoughts for Reflection

+ Consider the mighty arm of God stretched over you to protect you. Sing or recite Psalm 98, rejoicing in God's protection as Mary rejoiced in God's wondrous deeds.

+ Name the monsters that trouble your inner self. Pray the Magnificat with Mary, entering into her attitude of confidence in the power of God's protection.

- Pray the Lord's Prayer today asking that those who go into dangerous situations to rescue the victims of disaster or who minister to the needs of refugees may be "delivered from evil."
- Consider that God's strong arm overshadows those who suffer persecution for the sake of justice. Stand in solidarity beside them under this protective shadow.
- Reflect upon the events and issues of the day. What promotes the common good? Stand under the mighty arm of God and speak out for that which promotes human dignity for the least among us.

## Additional Scripture for Reflection

I will rescue you by my outstretched arm and with mighty acts of judgment (Ex 6:6).

I will make my justice come speedily;
my salvation shall go forth
and my arm shall judge the nations (Is 51:5).

With your arm you redeemed your people (Ps 77:16).

Your strong arm scattered your foes (Ps 89:11).

## Prayer

God of compassion, you led your people into freedom. I invite you into my life. Lead me to inner freedom and wholeness. Direct my steps on the path to which you are calling me. Give me eyes to see where you are at work drawing all people into your kingdom. Give me ears to hear your word. Give me the will and courage to follow you wherever you might lead.

Mary, Mother of the poor, Mother of refugees, Mother of the oppressed, show me the way of compassion for all who suffer. Teach me how to respond to the needs of others as you would respond. Pray to the Holy Spirit for me that I might act with wisdom in discerning God's will and live in accord with it. Pray for me that I might be united with Jesus, your son, as I journey toward the fullness of God's reign.

# Scattering the Proud

God has confused the arrogant in the conceit of their hearts.

*Mary*, a faithful daughter of Israel, stands at the head of a line of women who preceded her in singing songs of praise and thanksgiving for liberation from oppression. Miriam, the sister of Moses, praised God for the deliverance of her people from slavery in Egypt after crossing the Red Sea (Ex 15:21). Hannah, the mother of Samuel, sang of God breaking the power of the mighty and reversing the condition of the poor (1 Sam 2:4-8). The Song of Deborah (Jgs 5) and the Song of Judith (Jdt 16:1-17) celebrate God's protection and intervention in the vanquishing of enemies who oppressed their people. In Mary's Song, however, there is no rejoicing in the defeat of enemies. Mary rejoices in God's salvific action which liberates and brings all into right relationships within the kingdom of God.

"God has confused the arrogant in the conceit of their hearts," Mary sings out. The line could also be translated, "God has scattered the proud in the conceit of their hearts." In scripture, the *heart* is the center of one's inner life. Who are the proud ones that God has scattered? In the time of Mary, they might have been considered the enemies of Israel whom God overthrew with the might of his arm. Pride characterized the enemies of Israel who presumed to rule over what belonged to God (Jer 48:29). The unfaithful people of Israel who did not live according to the covenant were considered proud. In the psalms there are references to enemies of the righteous ones who are called proud, arrogant, or insolent. In the Book of Job, the pride that puts one in conflict with God is intellectual (Jb 38:15).

In the New Testament, the proud or arrogant are in opposition to the lowly. The scribes and Pharisees are arrogant in their criticism of Jesus for associating with outcasts, healing on the sabbath, and forgiving sins (Lk 6:17-32). Antagonism to Jesus' actions seems to have caused them to miss the point of his message. The apostles Peter and James admonish the early Christians to be humble in their dealings with one another, warning them that "God resists the proud and bestows his favor on the lowly."

Pride or arrogance is the first of three forces opposed to God and to the lowly ones who are the recipients of God's mercy. There are three human greatnesses or self-sufficiencies: pride, power, and riches. Surprise! We are facing a paradox here. Are not a position of honor and prestige, the power to control, and access to resources for a comfortable life the very things to which people aspire? Are these not the things that liberate? The mass media has given us the message of what we must do and possess to look good, feel good, and be happy. Mary's message of God's manner of acting doesn't fit with what we hear day to day in our society.

In a great saving act, God is bringing about a reversal of the situation of the proud, powerful, and wealthy. Even if we count ourselves among the humble, poor, and powerless, this may not immediately strike us as good news, especially if we are endeavoring to join the ranks of the privileged. In biblical terms, the heart is the center of human thought and intention. In the innermost thoughts of our hearts, down in the core of our being, we touch our deepest desires. Do we not desire good for ourselves and for those we love? To what does the intention to achieve good lead us? The key to reflecting upon Mary's words is to enter into the heart of the Almighty and to discover there God's compassion for all people.

God wills the ultimate good for all persons of every nation, race, and tongue—all persons without exception; that is, God wills the common good. Mary proclaims God's action in enhancing the dignity of the lowly, leveling the field of power, closing the gap between the haves and have-nots. Wherever God is at work bringing about the ultimate good of all, we find God's kingdom. When Jesus was asked when the reign of God would come, he responded, "The kingdom of God is among you" (Lk 17:21).

If we take the gospel seriously, we must look beyond what we are conditioned to believe we need to be happy. Jesus preached a way to happiness in the blessings and woes of the sermon on the plain. "Blessed are you poor, you who hunger, you who weep, you who are persecuted"(Lk 6:20-26). Entering into the paradox of the beatitudes gives us cause to think deeply about their meaning. In Luke's gospel the beatitudes are Jesus' four-step program to happiness. Clues to the presence of God's reign are there. The reversal of fortunes which is characteristic of the reign of God begins with the humbling of the proud, whose attitude brings them in conflict with the values of the kingdom.

Humility is the ability to perceive the truth of who we are in the light of who God is. Pride blocks this perception. More than anything else it is an exalted, but false, notion of who we are and to what we are entitled that blinds us to truth. Acting on these false notions leads in the end to the confusion and downfall of the arrogant.

With the clear eye of humility, Mary's vision is expansive. She proclaims the truth of who God is for herself and for all others of every generation who "fear the Lord." The way God has acted in the past in the Exodus from Egypt and the establishment of the covenant on Sinai points to how God is acting in the present for the welfare of all. The limited vision of the self-centered misses God's action in the "now" moment.

Within the kingdom the whole community is blessed by the humble attitude that a person holds toward God, inasmuch as this humility finds expression in the person's attitude toward others. The common good is best served where individuals are able to engage in dialogue, listening carefully to others' ideas as well as presenting their own. Some creative and original thinkers who were influential in leading others into new ways of thinking showed themselves remarkably open to listening to less knowledgeable people criticize and find fault with their ideas.

In his study of the Magnificat, the pioneer of modern biblical interpretation, Pere Marie-Joseph Lagrange, considered the pride that puts one in conflict with God to be intellectual. Intellectual pride is an affliction to which more than scholars are prone. Who has not met someone so absolutely convinced that his or her idea is the only right one that no opposing idea can even be heard? My own nightmare is to inquire, "Who comes to mind when the words *arrogant* or *proud* are mentioned?" and to hear the response, "Well, actually, it's you." Then my equanimity flies out the window on the wings of self-righteous indignation. Self-righteous indignation was an affliction of the Pharisees who opposed Jesus' message. Self-righteous adherence to one's ideas to the exclusion of consideration of any other is a stumbling block to arriving at truth in any situation.

It takes humility to admit to being wrong and to stretch one's thinking to embrace new information. The old saying, "A man convinced against his will is of the same opinion still," can apply to both men and women. The danger is to be so stubbornly attached to our own opinions that we miss the truth in a situation altogether. There can be no resolution of conflict when both sides are self-righteously convinced that no middle ground is possible. On the other hand, it takes courage to stay the course when, after all sides of an issue have been presented and openly considered, one in good conscience concludes that the evidence of truth is on his or her side. In resolving conflicts, the goal is the common good. We seek to find benefits for all sides of a controversy, to establish a just solution that assures future peace.

From petty family squabbles to political controversies to international conflicts, we see the need for negotiating peace. We cringe at the arrogance of those who promote the senseless slaughter of whole groups of defenseless people in order to gain a political advantage. Reports of atrocities in places like Guatemala, El Salvador, Bosnia, Kosovo, East Timor, Chiapas, Northern Ireland, and other lands dominate the international news. Yet, "God has confused the arrogant in the conceit of their hearts," Mary sings out. Weary of war, we wish the reign of God would manifest itself in our midst now, today.

The clear vision of the humble sees the reign of God in the actions of peacemakers, in those who care for the victims of violence, in those who help rebuild war-torn areas, in those who educate others in the ways of nonviolent resolution of conflict, in leaders such as Nelson Mandela who are willing to suffer for a long time in the cause of justice, in those wronged who reject bitterness and the taking of revenge. The message of Jesus to forgive wrongs, to love our enemies, and to do good to those who hate us is the most difficult lesson of the gospel. Those who are able to do so must surely confuse the arrogant in the conceit of their hearts. In so doing, we are acting most like God, whose love embraces all.

# Thoughts for Reflection

✦ You have been loved into existence by the Creator. From no one you became someone because of God's choice. In a quiet moment of reflection, look into the depth of your heart. Ask God to reveal to you the truth of who you are. Embrace this truth. If you find chaos and confusion within, ask for healing.

✦ Pray the Lord's Prayer slowly today, pausing over the words, "Forgive us our trespasses as we forgive those who trespass against us." Whom do you need to forgive? From whom do you need to ask forgiveness? Ponder that Jesus asked forgiveness for those who crucified him.

✦ In times of prayer when scattered thoughts rage about you as the winds of a hurricane, focus upon the still point in the eye of the storm and enter into God's presence there.

✦ In the city of Dayton, Ohio, there is a group of people who gather at places where violent actions have taken place. They come together to pray for both victims and perpetrators, to bless the site and make it a place of peace. Consider planning some kind of group response to violence in your own area.

✦ Edith Stein knew the horror of Nazi arrogance. As the dark clouds of the holocaust swirled around her, she reflected upon the mystery of God's presence in the midst of this evil. Consider this portion of her poem, "Aphorisms in the Month of June 1940."

III.
From night to light who'll be our guide?
How will the horror end?
Where will the sinners be justly tried,
When will our fortunes mend?

From the Mount of Olives His anguished plea
To the Father in Heaven He hurled.
His agony gained Him the victory,
Determined the fate of the world.
There prostrate yourselves and pray, and then
Ask no more: Who? How? Where? or When?

IV.
Judge not lest you be judged in turn,
Appearances cloud our view,
We guess at the truth, but only learn
God alone knows the truth.[7]

## Additional Scripture for Reflection

I will put an end to the pride of the arrogant,
    the insolence of tyrants I will humble (Is 13:11).

When pride comes, disgrace comes;
    but with the humble is wisdom (Prv 11:2).

"God resists the proud, but gives grace to the humble"
(Jas 4:6).

"God opposes the proud
    but bestows favor on the humble."
So humble yourselves under the mighty hand of God,
that he may exult you in due time (1 Pt 5:5).

# Prayer

Lord, you promised to send your Spirit to your followers. Trusting in your love and compassion, I claim this promise and invite you into my inner being today. Be present with me as I go about my tasks. Spirit of truth, make me open to seeking the truth in all things. Let your truth shine upon me when I experience inner confusion and chaos. Bring to light all that I need to know to act justly and compassionately. Save me from the pride or arrogance that clouds my understanding. Glory to you, Spirit of truth and love.

Mary, woman of truth, with wide vision you perceived God's action, visible and invisible, drawing all into the reign of justice, truth, and love. Pray for me that I, too, may perceive where God is at work in the world today and may have the will and courage to enter into this action. God's kingdom come. God's will be done.

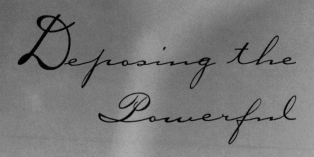

# Deposing the Powerful

---

## God has pulled down the powerful from their thrones, and lifted up the lowly.

---

*T*he title "daughter of Zion" is a personification of the humble, devout people of Israel who are to be raised up at the coming of the messianic age. This title is applied to Mary as representative of those faithful Jewish people who will be lifted up by God. The pattern of the reversal of fortunes characteristic of the reign of God continues in verse 52 of Mary's Song. The upside-down nature of the kingdom of God is revealed once again, as the proud who put their trust in princes and powerful ones are confused in their hearts by God's action for the lowly. In a leveling of the social situation, God has deprived the powerful of their base of oppressive power and drawn the marginalized, powerless, and oppressed into the realm of control over their own lives.

As God has acted in the past in bringing the people out of a condition of slavery in Egypt, God is now doing and will do in the future. Away from the eyes of the powerful, the greatest liberator of all is formed in secret in Mary's womb. Mary's "yes" to God in welcoming the child of promise into her womb is a "yes" to God's saving action in history. By calling herself a humble servant of the Lord, Mary places herself among the faithful, lowly people who remain steadfast in their covenant relationship with God. Her son is to be named *Jesus*, in Hebrew, *Josuah*, meaning "Savior." As mother of Jesus and daughter of Zion, Mary embodies the people of the covenant from whom the Savior is to be born. Her "yes" to God is a "no" to all oppression.

The powerful that are spoken of in Mary's Song are rulers or officials who do not do God's will. Oppression of the people by those who should be concerned for their welfare is a manifestation of the breaking of the covenant relationship with God. They are removed, pulled down, or dethroned. This overthrowing of tyrants is a clear sign of God's power at work in history. In contrast to God's action against the powerful is God's action for the lowly. These are the *anawim*. The scriptural meaning of the word carries the concept of those who are small, lowly, bowed down, insignificant. In Mary's day the term *anawim* included a wide range of people who were poor and oppressed, whether in material ways or in spirit. Historically, oppression may be that caused by a foreign, political, or military power (Jdt 16:11, 1 Mc 14:14), or it may be that caused by the rich and mighty within Israel itself (Am 2:7, Is 58:4).

In his book *The Poor of Yahweh*, Albert Gelin looks at the evolution of the vocabulary of poverty in Hebrew literature. What began as denoting a social reality came to have a religious meaning, expressing a right attitude of soul in relationship to God. In the seventh century BCE, the prophet Zephaniah described the coming "Day of Yahweh" as a day of judgment, desolation, and destruction for the rich, proud, and powerful. The humble were instructed to seek justice and take shelter in the Lord. Those opposed to God were to be removed from the midst of the people. But a remnant people, humble and lowly, would be left in Jerusalem. These *poor of Yahweh* would be saved from disaster and gathered into a holy people, restored and made renowned (Zep 2–3).

It was this remnant people, called to be faithful to the covenant, that Zephaniah personified as daughter of Zion (Zep 3:12-15). These formed the community of the lowly with whom Mary identifies and whom she represents. It is a community characterized by poverty of spirit as well as material poverty. Such people as these are the poor who will inherit the kingdom of God in the beatitudes of the gospels. In Matthew 5:3 we read, "Blessed are the poor in spirit, for theirs is the kingdom of God." Luke 6:20 reads, "Blessed are you who are poor, for the kingdom of God is yours." The poor recognize their dependency upon God, cry out to God in their need, and are the recipients of God's salvation.

Mary's words depicting the action of God in lowering the proud and exalting the humble, dethroning the powerful and empowering the lowly, feeding the hungry and sending the rich away empty are dramatic. They appeal to our sense of distributive justice. We like to see the underdog win. This is God's action. Right on, God! Way to go! In reality the action of God is subtle, usually taking place behind the scenes of what is immediately evident. A Magnificat spirituality holds the strong conviction that God is at work bringing about the final victory over all forces that oppress and diminish those he loves. A sign of the presence of the reign of God, that is, where God is acting, is wherever people are striving to establish a political and social situation of just relationships in keeping with God's will.

The twentieth century has seen more than its share of tyrannical dictators, subjugation of peoples, conflicts of war, and mass destruction of land and homes. The earth has soaked up the blood of innocent victims of violence in our age, as in every age. We have seen tyrants fall and new ones take their place. In the midst of our history of war and oppression, Mary's words still stand. God is bringing about the ultimate victory over all evil. We are invited to be part of the action in bringing about a just social situation where all are held in dignity and there is equitable distribution of power and resources. But it is dangerous to interpret the message of the Magnificat to mean fomenting or justifying a violent revolution which would take power from one group and give it to another, thus creating a new group of oppressed.

The expectation for God's salvific action in the Hebrew scriptures was political and religious liberation. Jesus took another stance—liberation from sin. Unless the sins of pride and greed for power and wealth are addressed, political liberation changes the appearance but not the substance of the social situation.

This does not mean that we are to be passive in the face of structures of injustice in the social realm. It means that action for justice is in keeping with the gospel when it flows from inner conversion of heart. In 1971, the world synod of bishops met to consider the mission of the people of God to further justice in the world. In the introduction to their subsequent document, *Justice in the World*, they wrote: "Action on behalf of justice and participation in the transformation of the world fully appear to us as a constitutive dimension of the preaching of the Gospel, or, in other words, of the Church's mission for the redemption of the human race and its liberation from every oppressive situation."

In courageously denouncing human rights abuses and military violence, Oscar Romero, Archbishop of San Salvador, incurred the hostility of powerful political, military, and hierarchical elements in El Salvador. His assassination while celebrating Mass in a convent on March 24, 1980, shocked the world. However, his memory lives on and continues to inspire those who reject violence and refuse to remain passive in the face of repression and abuse of power.

Those who struggle for justice in the social realm have entered into the salvific action of God only when their struggle in the political realm is in keeping with their inner struggle against the temptations of power, prestige, and material gain. Daniel Berrigan is an example of one who was willing to suffer imprisonment and humiliation to awaken a nation to the misuse of military power. He teaches that action for justice should be taken only after serious prayer and reflection and in solidarity with others. Action for justice must never be reckless or violent to persons.

Paulo Freire, in his work *Pedagogy of the Oppressed*, speaks eloquently of the need for educating those who are victims of exploitation and oppression in such a way that they do not take on the structures of thought or the structures of control of their oppressors. In claiming their own dignity, the exploited and oppressed begin to resist being dehumanized. In turn, when the bonds of oppression are lifted, the temptation to oppress others must be resisted. Both tyrants who oppress and their oppressed victims suffer dehumanization, and both need to regain their humanity. Mary's words call us to conversion of heart. Entering into Mary's disposition is both to know God's love and to enter into the paradox of God's action of pulling down and lifting up as all are drawn into the reign of justice.

It would be easy to be overwhelmed by the magnitude of saving the whole world. That is God's work. We participate in small ways as we are able. In our own day by day existence we are faced with opportunities to deal with the use and misuse of power. It is well to recognize and be knowledgeable about it. The famous words of Lord Acton are worthy of some reflection: "Power corrupts and absolute power corrupts absolutely." It has been said that power is like poison and needs to be spread around to make it less toxic. This is why there are checks and balances to power in democratic government.

There are circles of power to which we all belong. As Americans we are citizens of a powerful nation. We try to vote responsibly in order to invest the wisest and most honorable representatives with power to govern us. We are able to raise our voices in affirmation or protest over our leaders' decisions. This is our right. But as followers of Jesus, it is our mission to bring a gospel perspective to the political issues of our day. Do we recognize when or where our powerful, first world nation is exercising tyranny over third world nations? Are we supportive when our nation acts to exercise justice in support of oppressed peoples? Do we perceive the difference between acting on behalf of justice and acting in retaliation or revenge? Do we recognize the spiraling effects of meeting violence with violence? Do we speak out for nonviolent resolution of conflict? Do we recognize the signs of the reign of God in our world?

Tyranny has many faces. Hitler is gone, but the legacy of racism, anti-Semitism, homophobia, and other residues of his ideology are present in our midst. Stalin is gone, but the practice of controlling others through violence and fear remains in society. It is evident on the domestic level in abuse of spouses and children. For some, it is present in their workplace. In looking into our own hearts, we may find traces of sinful attitudes that we are quick to condemn in others. It is possible that until some incident brings them to our attention, we don't even know that destructive attitudes are within us. So the psalmist prays, "Cleanse me from my unknown faults" (Ps 19:13).

When the infant Jesus was brought to the temple forty days after his birth, the aged Simeon prophesied to Mary, "Behold, this child is destined for the fall and rise of many in Israel, and to be a sign that will be contradicted (and you yourself a sword will pierce) so that the thoughts of many hearts may be revealed" (Lk 2:34-35). Dr. Martin Luther King, Jr., provoked strong reactions of hate and fear from many church-going people when he led a civil rights march through a middle-class neighborhood in Chicago. The thoughts of many hearts were revealed that day.

It is often our spontaneous reaction to persons or events that reveals to us our deepest attitudes of heart. The Quakers have a saying that there is something of

God in every person. The ability to perceive this sacred presence in every human being is evidence of a transformed heart. Nurturing and cherishing the spark of God's life within ourselves, we become aware of our own dignity and power to resist being tyrannized. Respecting others as bearers of the divine life, we resist using our power to tyrannize others. We can be teachers and role models of tolerance in word and action.

Children are not born xenophobic or tyrannical, but they are quick learners. A small child might engage in a power struggle with his parents over whether or not he will eat the vegetables on his dinner plate. The way that this power struggle is resolved is a learning situation for the child. He may be learning tactics of negotiation, tactics of passive resistance, or tactics of tyranny. If he learns that those more powerful than himself can prevail by inflicting pain and shame, he may later be found hitting smaller children on the school playground or hurling insults at others.

Opportunities to teach and model respect for the innate dignity of every human person surround us. The coming of the reign of God is not under our control, but we are privileged to be called to be in solidarity with God's action in dethroning tyrants and lifting up the lowly. A "yes" to actions for justice is a "no" to oppression. Mary walks beside us in this work.

Mary, daughter of Zion, personification of the faithful, lowly remnant people of Israel, is in solidarity with all who are in any way oppressed, but Mary's "yes" to God has put her in solidarity also with God's action in bringing about the paradoxical social reversal which characterizes the messianic kingdom. Her mission is to bear the Messiah, who will begin God's reign of justice among all people. The early Christian church from which the Magnificat arises understood itself as commissioned to carry on the mission of Jesus. Today we are called to be in solidarity with that mission.

# Thoughts for Reflection

✦ Sit quietly with Mary pondering the words, "God has pulled down the powerful from their thrones, and lifted up the lowly." Enter into Mary's disposition as she speaks on behalf of all people who are oppressed. Pray for anyone you know is suffering oppression of any form.

✦ Look deeply into your heart and pray for insight concerning possession and use of power. Ask what power over self or others is under your control. How do you use the power you have?

✦ Consider that God desires your own freedom from oppression and fear. Image creative, loving ways to resist being diminished in dignity or manipulated by others for their gain.

✦ With Mary, stand in solidarity with those who lack power over their own lives and decision-making. Determine to speak up as an advocate for minorities and weaker members of society, such as children and the elderly, whenever the opportunity presents itself.

✦ Search out the services in your area that are available for victims of domestic violence. Educate yourself on this issue. Offer assistance if you are able.

✦ A number of peace and justice organizations welcome new members. Consider joining Pax Christi, Fellowship of Reconciliation (FOR), Amnesty International, Witness for Peace, or some other organization. FOR as well as Pax Christi publishes literature for adults and children on peacekeeping.

✦ Pray Psalms 34 and 35. Ask God's blessing upon our nation and pray that we will be sent leaders who will lead in the ways of wisdom, justice, and peace.

# Additional Scripture for Reflection

Shout for joy, O daughter Zion! (Zep 3:14).

The LORD makes poor and makes rich,
  he humbles, he also exalts (1 Sm 2:7-8).

Off with the turban and away with the crown! Nothing shall be as it was! Up with the low and down with the high! (Ez 21:31).

The thrones of the arrogant God overturns
  and establishes the lowly in their stead.
The roots of the proud God plucks up,
  to plant the humble in their place (Sir 10:14-15).

## Prayer

Lord, you know all things and order all things with wisdom. Give me your Spirit of Wisdom that I may discern the truth in all things. Give me insight to see the source of my own power and the will to use it for good. Guide the events of my life today that I may treat all those with whom I come in contact as bearers of your presence. Bless and protect the most powerless among us.

Mary, Mother of the homeless, Mother of the ridiculed and disdained, Mother of the powerless little ones, Mother of the elderly and infirm, Mother of students who are shamed by failure, Mother of the victims of violence and repression, Mother of those who live in fear, pray for us.

# The Hungry and the Rich

---

God has filled the hungry with good
things,
and the rich he has sent
away empty.

---

The core message of the second part of Mary's Song is
the paradox of social reversal in the reign of God. Mary
has proclaimed God's action against the proud and powerful and for the humble and lowly. Now it is the situation of the rich that is reversed as the hungry poor are
filled with good things and those whose greed caused
their situation of need are sent away empty.

The contrast between the fate of the hungry and that of
the well-fed has a precedent in the Song of Hannah (1 Sm
2:5), but for the most part in the Hebrew scriptures physical hunger is not considered a blessing. The blessing of a
fruitful land and abundant food is a reward promised to
those who keep the covenant (Lv 26:5; Dt 28:4). Spiritually,
hunger for the word of God is a judgment which is a

gnawing lack of everything that gives life (Amos) or is a figurative expression for religious longing (Sirach). Psalm 107 praises God because "he satisfied the longing soul and filled the hungry soul with good things."

In Luke's gospel, however, Jesus calls the hungry "blessed" (6:21) and pronounces "woe" to those who are filled (6:25). The parable of the rich man and Lazarus (16:19-31) serves to further illustrate a sinful situation of injustice where the callousness of the rich man allows for the hunger of Lazarus. Worse still, the rich man seems not to even notice Lazarus at his gate. The condition of Lazarus seems not to have been a concern to him. Jesus does not give a reason for Lazarus' hunger, only stating the fact of his misery. It is dogs who are portrayed as compassionate, for they lick the hungry man's wounds.

In the parable, no other sins are attributed to the rich man except his disregard for Lazarus. It is only in the afterlife that the rich man becomes aware of Lazarus as a person loved by God and worthy of receiving a comfortable place among the ancestors while the rich man is in torment. What a surprise this reversal of fortunes must have been. It is even too late to warn his brothers who are in danger of suffering the same fate. If they did not listen to the prophets, they would not listen to anyone, even if someone appeared from the abode of the dead to alert them, the rich man is told.

Eight centuries before Christ, the prophet Amos, in fiery rhetoric, denounced the greed of those who disregarded the social situation of poverty, who even engaged in fraud to cheat the poor of what was justly theirs. This trampling upon the poor was a breaking of the covenant with God and would be punished by famine—famine from hearing the word of the Lord (Am 8:4-14). Isaiah also warns the wealthy rulers who crush the unfortunate and grind down the poor when they look for help (Is 3:14-15). They are to suffer the loss of their riches. Isaiah's call is for awareness. Complacency in riches has rendered the wealthy blind and deaf to God's action in their midst and to God's word. The word of the Lord calls them back to observance of the law of the covenant and its mandate for social justice.

Does God reject the rich? Of course not! God loves all people. The reversal of fortunes of the greedy rich and the hungry poor is therapeutic. The rich need to be awakened to the structures of injustice in society that hold the poor in a cycle of poverty. All are called into the reign of God, a reign of true justice. A social structure in which the rich continue to get richer as the poor get poorer is headed for disaster. The prophets cut through apathy and complacency with the power of their words. They energize the people with a message of hope. When the conscience is awakened to the demands of justice, the land is restored and prosperity returns.

The reversal of fortunes between the rich and the hungry poor, which is due to the salvific action of God and is praised in the Magnificat, sets the tone for a major theme in Luke: God's favor to the poor. That God should provide us with our daily bread is a petition of the Lord's Prayer (11:3), as is a plea for the coming of the "kingdom of God"(11:2). Luke has put upon the lips of Mary a great proclamation of the coming reign of God. Mary participated in God's action of drawing all into the kingdom of peace, justice, and love by accepting the mission to which God called her. The Jewish Christian church at Jerusalem was the probable home of Mary after the death and resurrection of Jesus. This is the church from which the Magnificat arises. It was a church of mission.

Mary's proclamation that God has "filled the hungry with good things and sent the rich away empty" is a prophetic call to awareness. The hungry who are filled with good things are those who hunger for God and for the situation of justice to which God's love impels them. God comes to those who desire the divine presence in proportion to that desire. Empty of greed, self-centeredness, and distractions, we create space in our hearts, souls, and minds which can be filled by God. The peril of the rich is the sad situation of being so filled with self-interest that there is little room to be filled by God's presence and so busy that there is little time for silent attention to God's voice.

Mary's words are also a call to action. A sign of the presence of the reign of God is a political and social situation of just relationships in keeping with God's will, where there is no hunger among the many because of the greed of a few. We participate in the mission of Jesus by working to transform structures of society that create hunger. This includes a concern for our home, Earth. Land is the greatest material resource given us by our Creator, and its bounty is meant for all its inhabitants. Practices that protect the ecological health of our soil, water, and air will ensure that future generations may eat of the land's produce.

The New Testament scholar Raymond Brown stated that poverty and hunger of the oppressed in the Magnificat are primarily spiritual. The early Christian community at Jerusalem, however, knew real poverty. They lived in a land occupied by a foreign power to which they were required to pay taxes. For these early Christians, the good news was that the ultimately blessed are not the mighty and rich.

Then, as today, the mission of the church was one with the mission of Jesus in bringing about the fullness of God's reign. Mary, who stood at the point of the inbreaking of the messianic era into human history, is the inheritor of all the national aspirations and hopes of the people of Israel, who remember how God acted to liberate them from oppression in the past. In images and language from the Hebrew scriptures, she expresses the sentiments of the New Israel, the people who have experienced the salvific action of God in the person of Jesus. Having received the Holy Spirit together with Mary (Acts 2:4), the followers of Jesus recognize that the promise made to Abraham is not only being fulfilled in their midst but will be extended to all those who are called (Acts 2:39). The mission of the church continues the mission of Jesus to bring all into the reign of God. This is the reign of true justice.

Our spirituality is lived out in our lifestyle, in our service for others, in the causes we support, and in the political choices we make. Entering into Mary's disposition as she is depicted by Luke enables us to view the circumstances of our own lives and the events about us with gospel lenses. This is not a comfortable perspective. It means that we look for truth in the vast amount of information that bombards us daily in the news media and in our personal contacts with others. It means that we are alert and aware to where God is acting to bring all into the kingdom of peace, justice, and love.

Dom Helder Camara, Archbishop of Recife and Olinda in Brazil's poverty stricken northeast, worked untiringly for social justice for the poor and for the recognition of human rights for all. In recognition of his work, he was four times nominated for the Nobel Peace Prize, but he never received the award. He spoke out against the abuses of the 1964–1985 Brazilian military dictatorship. For this he suffered revilement and scorn. When Archbishop Camara died in 1999 at the age of 90, he was greatly mourned by the poor. The oft-quoted remark about his work touches upon the paradox of working on behalf of social justice: "If I give food to the poor they call me a saint. If I ask why the poor do not have food, they call me a communist."

Generosity toward the hungry poor is evident in the many people who contribute their own resources and time to stock food pantries that distribute supplies to those in need. At Thanksgiving time and during other special holidays, some families share their meals with those who are far from their families, lonely, or poor. Churches and other agencies that run soup kitchens or collect food for poor families meet with a whole-hearted response when they call for donations. We do not want to see anyone hungry, either in our own homeland or in other countries. Our hearts are touched by pictures of hungry children. The gospel inspires us to be generous to others as God is generous to us.

There is no lack of good will; neither is there a lack of land or resources on our planet Earth to feed a hungry world. Why, then, are people hungry? Bread for the World, an organization which documents the political causes of hunger, calls malnutrition the hidden holocaust of our day. President Carter's *Commission on World Hunger* stated that the issue of ending world hunger comes down to political choice. Most basic to the cause of hunger in the world is poverty. The poverty of third world countries continues to increase as these countries find themselves sinking deeper and deeper into debt to the developed nations of the first world.

In undeveloped nations people who should have the ability to feed themselves often find their access to land for local food production blocked. The unequal distribution of productive land ownership where a few wealthy or ruling families or foreign corporations control vast tracts of land leave the dispossessed who work the land no voice in how the land is used. Agricultural techniques that deplete soil of its nutrients are sometimes used to produce cash crops for export. This mining of the soil deprives future generations of sustainable resources to feed themselves. Land reform and fair trade practices are political choices.

War also devastates the land, creating large populations of refugees who can neither plant nor harvest. Farm animals are killed and mines on farm land make it hazardous for farmers who do return to work their fields. Financial resources poured into the production and purchase of weapons of war leave poorer nations without the means of financing agricultural and social development. War is a political choice.

Abusive exploitation of the world's forests, grasslands, croplands, water supplies, and fisheries contributes to the depletion of these important food resources. Conservation is a political choice.

Globalization of the economy complicates the food production and distribution situation. Small family farmers, long the backbone of sustainable food production and vital rural communities, find it difficult to compete in a world market and are fast disappearing from the agricultural scene. Cheap labor is sought. The rich then eat the bread earned by the labor of the poor while the poor go hungry. Just wages and working conditions for those who labor on the land and in factories is a political choice.

As a child, I questioned the feasibility of sending my cold oatmeal to a hungry child in a far off country. As an adult, I know that it is only in solidarity with others that a transformation of social structures can be achieved. We are locked together on a limited planet with limited resources. Individually, we can limit our own consumption of resources, engage in good ecological practices, and educate ourselves about ways to reduce world hunger. Networking with others, we can become involved in action against hunger. It is possible to reduce world hunger if there is a political will to do so.

The psalms are filled with expressions of gratitude to God for the gift of land and for the bounty it provides. The law in Israel instructed reapers to leave behind a portion of the harvest for the poor to glean for their sustenance. This was not charity but justice. In the gospel of Matthew, those who hunger and thirst for justice are called blessed (Mt 5:6). Hunger for a just society in which there is no malnutrition among the many due to the greed of a few is as much a religious longing as the longing for God.

Starvation of the spirit may be less evident to us than physical hunger, yet it is widespread in our midst. Hungers of the human heart include: the desire for freedom from fear and loneliness; the desire for freedom to make choices about our lives; the desire for wholeness of body and spirit; the longing for family and friends to fill the open spaces in our hearts; the quest for knowledge to fill the emptiness of our minds; the yearning for a place to belong where we are accepted and loved. Beneath these hungers is the longing for God. "You have made us for yourself, O Lord, and our hearts are restless until they rest in you," St. Augustine wrote.

It is the space of hunger for God that God hungers to fill. Loneliness for God creates the emptiness within to accommodate our divine guest. The spiritual writer Henri Nouwen once spoke of loneliness as a deep wound in the human soul. He then compared it to the Grand Canyon, a great wound in the earth's surface, yet majestic and beautiful. Empty of the cravings for wealth, power, and fame, there is room for the Holy One. Empty of tireless striving for riches, positions of prestige and control, there is time to attend to real values, to the things of God. Embrace the void within your heart. It is there God calls to you.

Mary, the lowly servant of God, was filled with the greatest of good things. She bore the child of promise, who would preach the good news of God's love for the hungry poor, the outcasts, the downtrodden, those lonely and forgotten. In league with Mary, we, too, carry the presence of God within us. To fill hungry bodies and hungry hearts is a holy work.

## Thoughts for Reflection

---

+ Seek out a quiet space to sit and reflect for a given number of minutes. Attempt to empty your mind and let go of distractions. It may not be easy at first. Be gentle with the distractions. Let them simply float away. Keep coming back to focus on your empty, inner space. Above all, do not let yourself feel guilty about doing nothing. This is prayer.

Imagine Mary sitting beside you. Make a gesture of handing her your plans for the day, your fears, anxieties, and other distractions. Ask her to hold them for you during your time of inner focus. Silently yearn for God to fill you, but do not use words.

Go deep into your heart and touch the place of your greatest longing. This desire may be exactly what God desires for you. After your time of prayer, write down that longing and return to it when you have time during the rest of the day. Before you retire for the night, remember the desire. Is it still your deepest longing? Place it in God's heart while you sleep.

✦ Share a meal with someone who is hurt or lonely. Feed the spirit as well as the body.

✦ Take time to make the blessing before meals a meaningful prayer. Ask God's blessing upon the land and those who work upon it.

✦ In the eucharist Christ shares himself as food. Both rich and poor share in this one meal. The following prayer acknowledging the divine presence in the eucharist was written by Thomas Aquinas:

O Sacred Banquet in which Christ is received,
the memory of his passion is recalled,
the soul is filled with grace and
the pledge of future glory is given us.

## Additional Scripture for Reflection

Blessed are you who are now hungry,
for you will be satisfied (Lk 6:21).

Woe to you who are filled now,
for you will be hungry (Lk 6:25).

Blessed are they who hunger and thirst for
 righteousness,
  for they will be satisfied (Mt 5:6).

Yes, days are coming, says the Lord God,
  when I will send famine upon the land:
Not a famine of bread, or thirst for water,
  but for hearing the word of the Lord (Am 8:11).

He who eats of me will hunger still,
  he who drinks of me will thirst for more (Sir 24:20).


## Prayer

O God, thank you for the blessings of land and water from which we obtain our food. Bless those who labor to bring it to our tables. Keep me ever mindful of your love for all people, rich and poor. You fed the hungry with manna from heaven. You satisfy the hungry hearts of those who call on you. I call upon you now to open my heart to all who are in need. For those who are hungry today, I pray, "Give us this day our daily bread." I ask this in the name of your son, Jesus.

Mary, Mother of the poor and of those who hunger, walk beside me today. Teach me the way of compassion for all who hunger. Pray for me that the presence of the Holy Spirit who dwells within me may touch the lives of those with whom I come in contact and give them joy.

# God's Servant

> God has come to the help of his
> servant Israel,
> remembering his mercy.

Like a father or mother guiding the footsteps of an unsteady child, the Almighty One reached out to grasp the hand of Israel, God's cherished servant. In the final verses of the Magnificat, the principal reasons for Mary's praise are summarized into one great fact: the salvation event has taken place. The coming of the messiah, the child of promise, was a central event in religious history. It was not an instantaneous curing of all the ills of humanity or an instantaneous conquering of all forces of evil. It was the beginning of the end time when the reign of God would come in fullness and all evil would be conquered.

Christians call this end time the *parousia*. The early Christian community of believers, poor and persecuted, looked forward with hope and longing for the *parousia* when Christ would return and gather all into the fullness of the reign of joy and gladness in God's presence. As the years passed, they began to understand that their time was an in-between time, and this time between the first and second coming of Jesus was a time of service. It was a time to act in the spirit of Jesus, spreading the good news of God's love to all peoples and nations.

In Luke's writing, Mary's voice rises from the midst of this earliest group of Jewish disciples of Jesus, the Jerusalem community. Mary, as daughter of Zion, personified the Jewish *anawim,* the faithful remnant of Israel. In the final verses of her song, her voice becomes the collective voice of the Christian *anawim* who saw themselves as the faithful remnant of Israel. Hope hinged upon their trust in God's *hesed*, his absolutely faithful, merciful, covenant love. God, whom Jesus called *Abba*, "Father," remembers mercy and acts according to his promise.

Yet, this small group of disciples was not to wait passively for God's final act. They was called to participate in God's action of drawing all into the kingdom. Their mission was to continue the mission of Jesus. This is the mission of the church, and our mission also. Luke places Mary in the midst of the women and men awaiting the fulfillment of Jesus' promise to send the Holy Spirit to guide and strengthen them (Acts 1:14). With the coming of the Spirit, the disciples were engulfed in the flames of God's love and empowered to enkindle this love in others. With courage and conviction they left the upper room where they were gathered, filled with the Holy Spirit and ready to serve the mission of Jesus to draw all into the reign of God.

The Magnificat contains a servant theme. In verse 48, Mary calls herself God's *doulas*, which is translated "servant" or "slave girl." In verse 54, Israel is called *paidos*, a child slave or servant.

A suffering messianic figure appears in the Servant Songs of the prophet Isaiah (42:1-4; 49:1-7; 50:4-11; 52:13–53). Here Israel is personified as a servant who bears the guilt of the people yet remains faithful to God's will in the midst of suffering, rejection, and humiliation. In the servant's steadfast obedience to God, he acts redemptively on behalf of all. The final verses of Isaiah 53 describe the servant's sacrificial death and ultimate triumph.

The early Christians attributed the Servant Songs to Jesus and understood themselves as God's servants in continuing the mission of Jesus. "Whoever wishes to be great among you will be your servant," Jesus told his disciples, "whoever wishes to be first among you will be the slave of all." He then reminded them that he had come, "not to be served but to serve and to give his life as a ransom for many"(Mark 10:43-45). The Christian church is a servant church. In 1965, Vatican II affirmed this in its document *Gaudium et Spes*, teaching that the role of the church is to carry on the work of Christ, who came to serve and not to be served.

Today, we are two millennia removed from the time of Mary's Song. What does it mean to be God's servant in the world in which we find ourselves? In his letter to the Romans, St. Paul tells us that we are God's servants and the reward for our service is a continuing growth in holiness until finally we attain eternal life (Rom 6:16-23). Eternal life is surely an offer we can't refuse. To direct our energies in the service of other individuals or in the service of the common good is a win-win activity. Those in need are helped, and the helpers win eternal life.

Christian tradition is filled with men and women whose experiences in prayer led them to be servants. They ascended the heights of holiness and left us as models of service. Catherine of Siena was given to understand in prayer that she could do no direct service to God but only to her fellow human beings. In her *Dialogue*, she recorded the Lord's words to her: "I have placed you in the midst of your neighbors: so that you can do for them what you cannot do for me, that is, love them without any concern for thanks and without looking for any profit for yourself. And whatever you do for them I will consider done for me."[8] How comforting this is to those who serve others without ever receiving a sign of gratitude, even perhaps receiving tokens of derision instead.

The fourteenth-century mystic Julian of Norwich was an anchorite. For perhaps fifty years she never ventured away from her anchor-hold, a small room attached to a church in Norwich. There she lived a life of prayer, and from her window, facing the street, she rendered the counsel for which she has became famous. In writing her "shewings" or visions, Julian tells a parable of a servant who desires to do the Lord's bidding but is overcome by human weakness and limitation. God does not blame the servant for this weakness but looks at the intention of the servant's heart. Julian also describes a delightful vision of heaven where the Lord is hosting a great feast and graciously thanking all his subjects for the service they have given.

The type of service that we render others is not as important as the quality of love which we bring to it. Service done in love is transformative. The attitude Jesus had toward the poor, the ill, the suffering, the outcasts of society shows us that every person has value. A scripture professor of mine once remarked that he would fear being in a world where there were no unfortunates who inconvenienced others by their need for care. "What would we become if there were no one to rescue us from our self-centeredness?" he wondered. The reward of the servant is sanctification on the way to eternal life.

Once, as a novice, I succumbed to a particularly vicious flu. I was embarrassed that others were burdened with doing my share of the work and apologized profusely for being an inconvenience to the novice who was our nurse. She cut short my complaint with, "It is my privilege to care for you. Thank you for giving me this opportunity." Graciousness in accepting service is as blessed as graciousness in giving it. It was a lesson I needed to learn.

What we are able to do as servants of the reign of God may seem insignificant, yet in solidarity with God's work we have a small part in the great things that lie beyond us. Archbishop Oscar Romero, who spoke out in defense of human rights and lost his life because of it, wrote the following:

> We accomplish in our lifetime only a tiny fraction of the magnificent enterprise that is God's work. Nothing we do is complete, which is another way of saying that the kingdom lies beyond us. It is not only beyond our efforts, it is even beyond our vision.

Mary, God's lowly servant, transformed by grace, bore the transforming presence of God to her cousin Elizabeth. Our most important service lies in bearing the transforming presence of the Holy Spirit who dwells within us to others. In this, Mary is our model of servanthood.

## Thoughts for Reflection

- ✦ Reflect today on Mary's claim to be God's servant (Lk 1:48). Mary expresses gratitude that God regards her lowly estate. Sanctify all the activities of your day by offering them in service to God.

- ✦ Mary bore the divine presence within her womb. Reflect upon the divine presence dwelling within you by grace. Embrace God's love for you.

- ✦ Mary, transformed by God's grace, was a transforming presence to Elizabeth and her child. Consider how your graciousness transforms others.

- ✦ Offer a prayer for those who serve you in any way. Thank them for their service when this is possible.

- ✦ Know your public servants. Call them to justice and integrity in decision-making. The common good is everyone's concern. Vote wisely for those who serve the common good.

✦ Read the Servant Songs in the book of the prophet Isaiah. They are found in 42:1-4; 49:1-7; 50:4-11; 52:13–53. These songs are good meditations for the season of Lent.

## Additional Scripture for Reflection

Here is my servant whom I uphold,
  my chosen one with whom I am pleased,
Upon whom I have put my spirit (Is 42:1).

You are my servant, he said to me,
  Israel, through whom I show my glory (Is 49:3).

For the Son of Man did not come to be served but to serve and to give his life as a ransom for many (Mk 10:45).

Though he was in the form of God . . .
  he emptied himself,
  taking the form of a slave,
  coming in human likeness (Phil 2:6, 7).

But now that you have been freed from sin and have become slaves of God, the benefit that you have leads to sanctification, and its end is eternal life (Rom 6:22).

# Prayer

Jesus, as Servant Messiah your whole life was lived in obedience to the will of the Father. You came not to be served but to serve. Love was the power with which you served. Send your Spirit to me that I may discern God's will for me. Purify the intentions of my heart that I may serve you today in serving others with love.

Mary, handmaid of the Lord, I look to you to teach me how to be God's servant. Walk beside me today. Assist me in my service and obtain for me the grace to see the presence of your son in everyone, especially in those with whom I find it most difficult to relate.

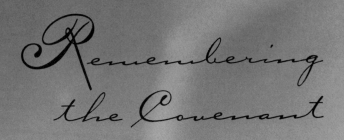

# Remembering the Covenant

> God has come to the help of his
> servant Israel,
> remembering his mercy,
> According to the promise he made to
> our ancestors,
> to Abraham and to his
> descendants forever.

The final verse of the Magnificat brings us back to the beginning of the great drama of salvation. God's action on behalf of his servant Israel is in fulfillment of his covenant. There is a connection between the saving action of God and his remembering. What God remembers is *hesed*—God's merciful, enduring, covenant love. The promise made to Abraham was sealed by a covenant, of which there are two accounts in Genesis. The promise was that Abraham should be the father of many descendants and that his progeny should inhabit a land of their own (Gn 15; 17). All that was asked of Abraham was faith in God. Abraham appears frequently in Luke; he is the spiritual father of Israel. The thought of Luke seems to be that the wealthy, the proud, and the powerful, or those in opposition to God's will for his people, have been eliminated from this spiritual community. But for those true descendents of Abraham, the faithful remnant people, God's mercy is forever.

In verse 49 of her song, Mary praises God for the wondrous things done for her. In verse 51, we hear her proclaim that God has shown might with his arm. The words are reminiscent of the Exodus and the Sinai covenant. The Sinai covenant was made between God and the people. This covenant required more than faith. It required observance of the law which dictated justice in human relations. Oppression of the poor and powerless was a breaking of the covenant.

A third covenant, the Davidic covenant, is recalled in the first chapter of Luke's gospel. In this covenant God promised that the house of David would endure forever. At the time of the annunciation (1:31-33), Mary is told by the angel Gabriel that the Lord God will give her son the throne of David. He will rule over the house of Jacob forever and his kingdom will have no end. This pronouncement, along with the allusion to the servant of the Lord in the Magnificat, establishes the messianic role of Mary's son. It would seem that the whole of the covenant relationship of God to Israel in constant, faithful love is summed up in Mary's Song.

God's remembering is efficacious and creative. What God has promised must come to be, for God is absolutely faithful. What God remembers is loving mercy. The language and images of the Magnificat carry within them the history of God's dealings with his elect. The covenant theology of first-century Judaism shines through. Mary's

God is the Lord, the God of Israel. She has personally experienced his mercy, his faithful justice and love. She remembers how the Lord has upheld Israel, his servant, ever mindful of covenant mercy. Remembering God's past deeds engenders hope in a future under God's protection.

Our scriptures contain the collective memory of the Jewish people's relationship to God as well as the stories of Jesus held in the memory of the early Christian communities. Memory is a powerful thing. Memory of a person or event in the past makes that person or event present to us once again. In celebrating Passover each year, the Jewish people become once again the liberated, chosen people of God. In celebrating the Lord's Supper, Christians remember the life, death, and resurrection of Christ and become, once again, present at the saving event. Over and over our liturgy calls us to remember what God has done for us. In this memory we rejoice and give thanks.

What God remembers is mercy. In remembering us, the floodgate of divine love pours over us. What do we remember? In the Lord's Prayer we ask God to "forgive us our trespasses as we forgive those who trespass against us." We are to forgive as God forgives. Suppose we prayed, "God remember us as we remember others"? What does it mean for us to remember as God remembers? Memories of God's goodness remind us that God is indeed acting in our lives. With God's help we came through past difficulties, and there is no reason to doubt that God will be there for us for whatever we face in the future. Positive memories of others increase our love and gratitude for the people who have graced our lives with their goodness.

Imagination plays a part in memory. In sharing a common memory, different versions are offered by participants in the same event. We remember what is meaningful to us, and the actual event can be colored by imagination. Once, years after becoming an adult, I shared a memory of a childhood event with my father. To my surprise, he remembered the event quite differently. My memory was of a sad, anxious, eight-year-old sitting on the floor before a Christmas tree which sparkled with lights on a snowy Christmas morning. No one else was present. My two brothers had succumbed to an epidemic of scarlet fever and were confined to a hospital for children with contagious diseases. I had the mumps and couldn't go out. Our house was quarantined, and my friends couldn't come in. There were gifts under the tree, but I didn't dare touch them until my parents returned from wherever they were. It was the early days of World War II, and there was talk that my father might go to war. What I remembered was sadness and loneliness.

My father was astonished at my memory. "You were never alone," he insisted, "Don't you remember your grandmother coming to stay with you while your mother and I went to Mass and then to the hospital?" Yes, I did remember it then. He spoke of how he remembered that Christmas. We remembered that six weeks later my brothers were home, I was well, my mother gave birth to twins, and my father's job was deemed important enough to national defense to keep him working on the home front. My new memory, then, was one of being well-loved, cared for, and very blessed, privileged to be safe in a world ravaged by war. My memory moved from sadness to gratitude. Gratitude for those who committed their lives to bring peace to the world remains with me. Memory has power.

Since our emotions are ruled by our minds, we may feel again the emotion that a person or event evoked in us. The memory of a loved one may elicit tears, or the memory of an embarrassing event may cause us to blush. Feelings such as joy, awe, fear, anger, shame, longing, loneliness, or love, to name a few, accompany memories. The song, "Memory," from the Broadway musical Cats was instantly a show-stopper, for it touched the audiences' experience of the power of memories.

Memories evoke emotion. Unhappy memories are part of the human condition. What we do with them is important to our emotional well-being. It may take a confessor or counselor to help us deal with the feelings of guilt, shame, fear or anger that accompany unhappy memories. A student once shared with me his way of dealing with the memory of a grievance. "I was playing the tape of this hurt over and over in my mind and getting more and more depressed," he said. "So I finally decided to ditch that tape, put in a new one, and get on with my life." Memory can be healed.

Just as Abraham and Sarah were Mary's ancestors in her faith, so we have our own ancestors. We are connected to a multitude of holy men and women who preceded us in our faith. Among them, surely, are parents, grandparents, great-grandparents, and so on, forming a line that stretches back many centuries. It is well to remember the blessings that have come to us from our ancestors. Membership in the communion of saints links us to all who have gone before us, and their witness of faith and holiness is our spiritual inheritance. Recalling to mind the lives of ancestors in our spiritual family is a way to remind ourselves that we are not alone in our spiritual quest but are surrounded by the example and prayers of the saints.

Remembrance of God's loving mercy lived in the national memory of Mary's people. When national memory is filled not with remembrances of God's goodness but with historical grievances, there cannot be peace. Our age has witnessed the violence and devastation that follows when one group of people is motivated by national memory to wreak vengeance upon another. Today, analyzing world events with a gospel understanding, we note that violence begets violence and once war starts it is difficult to contain. Images from around the world make us cringe in horror at the brutality inflicted upon defenseless people.

To attempt to right the wrongs of history by violent means results in spiraling ever deeper into an abyss of violence and destruction. Hatred and the desire for revenge cannot be beaten out of a national memory. What Jesus preached was forgiveness of enemies and conversion of the heart. The message of the Magnificat is that God is acting to bring about the reign of right relationships, the reign of justice, and, therefore, of peace. To be in solidarity with the action of God is to actively resist evil in a way that does not perpetrate more evil. Nonviolent resistance to injustice flows out of a spirituality that trusts God's presence in the work of bringing about the ultimate victory over all oppression.

God remembers promises of mercy. What do we remember?

## Thoughts for Reflection

- ✦ Think back upon the major events of your life. Remember how God was present in those events. Offer a prayer of gratitude for God's goodness.

- ✦ When negative memories of past grievances surface in your mind, let go of them as you would let go of a helium balloon. Let them drift away. Focus upon God's love.

- ✦ Reflect upon the faith of your ancestors. What is your spiritual inheritance?

- ✦ Macrina Wiederkehr has written an insightful book, *Gold in Your Memories*. Read it when you have time and mine the gold in your memories.

- ✦ Faith cannot be taught, it must be caught. Share your faith memories with a friend. Listen as another shares his or her faith memories with you.

# Additional Scripture for Reflection

I will remember my covenant with Jacob, my covenant with Isaac, and my covenant with Abraham (Lv 26:42).

Remember your compassion and love, O LORD;
    for they are ages old (Ps 26:6).

Thus he has shown the mercy promised to our
            ancestors,
    and has remembered his holy covenant,
the oath that he swore to our ancestor Abraham (Lk 1:72-73, NRSV).

"Jesus, remember me when you come into your kingdom." Jesus replied to him, "Amen, I say to you, today you will be with me in Paradise" (Lk 23:42-43).

The days are coming, says the LORD, when I will make a new covenant with the house of Israel . . . I will forgive their evildoing, and remember their sin no more (Jer 31: 31, 34).

## Prayer

Lord, in your kindness, remember me. Bring me to the fullness of life in your reign. Remember our nation and raise up leaders who will lead us in the ways of justice and truth. Remember your church and bless it with pastors who are wise and compassionate. Remember those who are most in need of your loving mercy today.

# Ancient Prayer to Our Lady

Remember, O most gracious Virgin Mary, that never was it known that anyone who fled to your protection, implored your help, or sought your intercession was left unaided. Inspired by this confidence I fly to you, O Virgin of Virgins, my Mother. To you I come, before you I stand sinful and sorrowful. O Mother of the Word Incarnate, despise not my petitions but, in your mercy, hear and answer me. Amen.

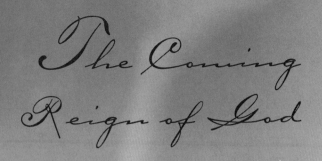

# The Coming Reign of God

*T*he message of the Magnificat is a message of hope. The mercy of God prevails. In the final analysis all will be well. All manner of things will be well. The reign of God is coming!

Mary's Song has echoed over two thousand years of Christianity, calling to us each evening at vespers to sing out in gratitude to God for our blessings, to put on the mind of Mary, and to enter into the dynamism of the coming of the reign of God, the reign of right relationships. Where do we find God's reign? Wherever God is acting on behalf of the people and we are participating in this action, there is the reign of God.

Two thousand years have passed and still in so many places the rich eat the bread produced by the labors of the poor. Where is the Holy One who fills the minds, hearts, spirits, and bellies of the hungry? Still thrones of nations are occupied by the mighty; swords and lances no longer shore them up, but fearsome and awesome weapons of mass destruction. Where is the strong arm of the Mighty One who pulls down the powerful and exalts the humble? Still the arrogant crush the hearts and spirits of those who are despised among us, the homeless, the mentally ill, victims of violence, the handicapped, the helpless young and elderly, those who we prefer not to see or think about. With the old rabbi of Elie Wiesel's story we ask, "Where is the mercy of God? Where is the God of mercy?"

Wherever the reign of God is found here today in our midst, there is the place where the poor are filled, the lowly are given dignity, the arrogant are confused, and warring parties are reconciled. Do we know this place? Do we, like Mary, have the wisdom to recognize the signs of God's reign here in our midst? Mary's Song is our song. May the wisdom of God dwell in us as it dwelt in Mary, that we, too, may have knowledge of divine things, recognize where God is at work, and be friends of God and prophets (Wis 7:27).

# Notes

1. Edward Schillebeeckx, *Mary: Yesterday, Today, Tomorrow*, p. 26.

2. Steven Payne, "Edith Stein, A Fragmented Life," *America*, October 10, 1998, p. 14.

3. Julian of Norwich, *The Revelations of Divine Love*, p. 92.

4. Thomas Merton, *Contemplative Prayer*, p. 70.

5. Jessica Powers, *The Selected Poetry of Jessica Powers*, p. 92. Copyright 1999 by Carmelite Monastary, Pewaukee, WI. Used with permission.

6. Raymond of Capua, *Life of Catherine of Siena*.

7. Susanne M. Batzdorff. *Edith Stein: Selected Writings*, pp. 74-75. Used with permission of Templegate Publishers, www.templegate.com.

8. Catherine of Siena, *Dialogue* #64.

# Bibliography

Batzdorff, Susanne M. *Edith Stein: Selected Writings*. With Comments, Reminiscences and Translations of Her Prayers and Poems by Her Niece. Springfield, IL: Templegate Publishers, 1990.

Byron, William. *The Causes of World Hunger*. New York: Paulist Press, 1982.

Camara, Dom Helder. *Spiral of Violence*. Trans. Della Couling. Kansas City, MO: Sheed and Ward, 1971.

Flannery, Austin P., OP (ed.). *The Documents of Vatican II*. Preface by John Cardinal Wright. New York: Costello Publishing Company, 1975.

Gebara, I. and M. Bingemer. *Mary, Mother of God, Mother of the Poor*. Trans. Phillip Berryman. Maryknoll, NY: Orbis Books, 1989.

Haughey, John C., SJ (ed.). *The Faith That Does Justice: Examining the Christian Sources for Social Change*. New York: Paulist Press, 1977.

Julian of Norwich. *The Revelations of Divine Love*. Trans. James Walsh, SJ. St. Meinrad, IN: Abbey Press, 1975.

Kappes, Marcianne. *Track of the Mystic: The Spirituality of Jessica Powers*. Kansas City, MO: Sheed and Ward, 1994.

Lagrange, Pere. *Personal Reflections and Memories*. Trans. Henry Wansbrough. Forward by Pierre Benoit. New York: Paulist Press, 1985.

Mattern, Evelyn. *Blessed Are You: The Beatitudes and Our Survival.* Notre Dame, IN: Ave Maria Press, 1994.

Merton, Thomas. *Contemplative Prayer.* New York: Image/Doubleday, 1990.

Metz, Johannes B. *Poverty of Spirit.* Trans. John Drury. Mahwah, NJ: Paulist Press, 1968.

Morneau, Robert F. *A Retreat with Jessica Powers: Loving a Compassionate God.* Cincinnati, OH: St Anthony Messenger Press, 1995.

Noffke, Suzanne. *Catherine of Siena: Vision Through a Distant Eye.* Collegeville, MN: The Liturgical Press, 1996.

Nolan, Mary Catherine, OP. *The Magnificat, Canticle of a Liberated People. A Hermeneutical Study of Luke 1:46-55, Investigating the World Behind the Text by Exegesis; The World in Front of the Text by Interpretive Inquiry.* Unpublished Dissertation. Dayton, OH: International Marian Research Institute, University of Dayton, 1995.

O'Brien, David J. and Thomas A. Shannon (eds.). *Renewing the Earth: Catholic Documents on Peace, Justice and Liberation.* Garden City, NY: Image Books, 1977.

O'Driscoll, Mary, OP. *Catherine of Siena: Passion for the Truth, Passion for Humanity.* Selected Spiritual Writings. New Rochelle, NY: New York City Press, 1993.

Peterson, Anna. *Progressive Catholicism in El Salvador During the Civil War and Today.* Archbishop Romero Lecture. Notre Dame, IN: Kellogg Institute, University of Notre Dame, 1998.

Powers, Jessica. *The Selected Poetry of Jessica Powers.* Regina Siegfried and Robert F. Morneau (eds.). Washington, D.C.: ICS Publications, 1999.

Prevallet, Elaine M. *Reflections on Simplicity.* Pendle Hill Pamphlet 244. Wallingford, PA: Pendle Hill Publications, 1982.

A Russian Pilgrim. *The Way of the Pilgrim.* Trans. Helen Bacovcin. Forward by Walter Ciszek, S.J. New York: Image/Doubleday, 1978.

Schillebeeckx, Edward. *Mary: Yesterday, Today, Tomorrow.* Trans. John Bowden. New York: Crossroad Publishing Company, 1993.

Soelle, Dorothee. *The Strength of the Weak: Towards a Christian Feminist Identity.* Trans. Robert and Rita Kimber. Philadelphia, PA: The Westminster Press, 1984.

Wiederkehr, Macrina. *Gold in Your Memories.* Notre Dame, IN: Ave Maria Press, 1998.